YOUNG KRISHNA

Francis G. Hutchins

Young Krishna

TRANSLATED FROM THE SANSKRIT

HARIVAMSA

Illustrated with paintings

from historic manuscripts

THE AMARTA PRESS

Other Books by Francis G. Hutchins

The Illusion of Permanence:
British Imperialism in India (1967)
India's Revolution: Gandhi and the
Quit-India Movement (1973)
Mashpee: The Story of Cape Cod's
Indian Town (1979)

Library of Congress Catalog Card Number 80-66834
ISBN: 0-935100-01-6

PUBLISHED BY
The Amarta Press
P.O. Box 202, West Franklin, New Hampshire 03235

Printed in the United States of America

TO ANN

Contents

Introduction

The story of Young Krishna was first told more than two thousand years ago. Originally recited by bards from memory, it was then written down sometime before the year 400 A.D. in the form preserved for us in the Sanskrit poem the *Harivamsa*. Since then the story of Krishna's youth has never stopped growing, and it remains today one of the most popular stories the world has ever known.

A person named Krishna probably lived in northern India about three thousand years ago, and probably took part as one among many noble chieftains in the great dynastic war which forms the subject of the twenty-five-hundred-year-old epic poem the *Mahabharata*. Then, about two thousand years ago, Krishna came to be thought of increasingly as the principal human incarnation of the god Vishnu and hence a definitive enunciator of religious truth. This is how Krishna is presented in the *Bhagavad Gita*, which is generally believed to be a somewhat late addition to the vast *Mahabharata* epic. As Krishna became more prominent, his relatively subordinate warrior's role in the battles recounted in the *Mahabharata* was supplemented by a new narrative in which Krishna was the central actor. Krishna's adult life, as chronicled in the *Mahabharata*, could not be made different, but the story of how Krishna grew to maturity was an epic that had not yet been told and of which Krishna himself could become the undisputed hero. First narrated in the shadow of Krishna's exploits as a dynastic warrior, the romance of Young Krishna in later centuries grew ever more remote from its historic origins. I have therefore chosen to translate the story of Krishna's youth as it is given in the oldest of the surviving versions. The *Harivamsa* subtly captures Krishna's dual character as epic hero and religious teacher. The *Harivamsa*'s account of Krishna's youth is both a tale of adventure and a way of expressing religious truth.

Readers of the *Harivamsa*'s story of Young Krishna may well respond simply to its narrative vitality, or to the pungency of its characterizations, or the accuracy of its portrayal of social and political realities, or to its elegance of poetic allusion. But appreciation of its purpose as a work of art calls for an awareness of its central vision. Put briefly, the story relates what happened when the eternal god Vishnu was born as a mortal human infant. Vishnu is worshiped by his followers as the supreme god, in fact as the only eternal god. His seat is fixed immovably in the highest heaven. He is never drawn to tilt vaingloriously across the sky with lesser gods. He need not assert himself at all. But because the earth is imperiled by the actions of a demon king, Vishnu leaves his high throne to be born as Krishna, a human child reared by nomadic cattle herders.

At first Krishna's amazing powers are hidden even from his foster parents, Nanda and Yasoda. Though a god, Krishna at birth cannot walk or talk. Some of his earliest feats —uprooting two trees, overturning a cart, killing a monstrous wet nurse —are, like many actions of ordinary children, unintentionally destructive. Krishna is astonishing, but still a child, and since all these miraculous accidents occur out of the herders' sight, only the effects of Krishna's energy are discovered as unexplained clues that this infant is somehow special. Krishna's first purposeful exercise of superhuman power occurs when he is about eight. To persuade the herders to move to better pastures and stop abusing the terrain where their cattle have grazed too long, Krishna creates murderous wolves who descend upon the settlement. Krishna wishes his elders well and in fact does know what is best for them, but they can hardly be expected to defer to the reasoning of one so young. So Krishna acts with a harshness common in young people, exerting covert intimidation by means of a pack of wolves.

The quelling of the serpent Kaliya shortly thereafter is Krishna's first overt demonstration of his marvelous powers. Kaliya, who is polluting the river on which the herders and their cattle depend for water, is subdued in full view of the assembled herder clan. The herders are finally convinced that Krishna must be a god of some sort, and his status among them is immediately changed. From the time he is eight or so, Krishna's rare power, if not his specific identity, is recognized by the herders. With humility, the herders acknowledge that whoever he may be, he is more powerful than they are and so must be respected. Krishna himself experiences no inner uncertainty; he knows he is Vishnu on earth. But the process by which Krishna's identity is gradually recognized by others is tense and dramatic. The people nearest Krishna try especially hard to understand him, straining earnestly to bring into focus the strangeness of this "human-not human" boy.

In ending Kaliya's contamination of the river, Krishna also foreshadows his ultimate earthly objective, the death of the demon king Kamsa, who is polluting the entire nation he rules by "making virtuous action difficult for everyone." Alone among the demons Krishna meets before taking on Kamsa, the serpent

Kaliya is described as himself a king and shown surrounded by wives and servants. Kaliya is the only one of these demons who is banished, not killed, which hints that he may have to be dealt with again.

In ways such as these, the story builds toward Krishna's final confrontation with Kamsa. Time after time Kamsa comes close to success in his attempts to destroy Krishna. If Krishna had been killed while still a boy, Vishnu would have returned to the heavens uninjured. Kamsa would have escaped his fate, at least for a time. In the end Krishna wins all his battles, but the vulnerable flesh-and-blood body that Vishnu's spirit temporarily inhabits incurs injury, and Krishna's triumphs are by no means always assured, especially in the eyes of his human friends. The killing of Kamsa by the youthful Krishna signals Krishna's triumphant attainment of young manhood and spreads throughout the entire nation the sense of awe and pleasure that Krishna's presence has already brought to the herders among whom he has spent his youth.

Kamsa's reign has brought turmoil to the kingdom of Mathura. The sincere cooperation that a good king can hope for from his subjects had been replaced by fear and consternation. Suspicious of well-meaning persons and contemptuous of all just norms of conduct, Kamsa has overturned the orderly procedures of government established by Ugrasena, whom Kamsa has forcibly expelled from the throne. In seizing Ugrasena's throne, Kamsa has in fact not simply ousted a royal father from power a bit early; Kamsa is doubly a usurper for, being of illegitimate birth, he has no hereditary right to the throne at all. Kamsa confesses to his elephant trainer that he is not really the son of Ugrasena but of a demon who has seduced Ugrasena's queen. It is typical of Kamsa that he should have revealed this secret to a low-minded elephant trainer. Kamsa surrounds himself with ruffians and hoodlums while scorning the worthier members of his realm.

That Kamsa would be rash enough to confess such an incriminating secret to anyone suggests, moreover, the basic turbulence of his mind. Kamsa lacks self-control. He succumbs to unpredictable moods. As bizarre as his confession to the elephant trainer is his sudden remorse for having killed his aunt Devaki's children. Kamsa begs Devaki's forgiveness with seeming sincerity but soon is once again acting as ruthlessly as ever. Inherently unstable and anxious, Kamsa fears everything. Any out-of-the-ordinary occurrence worries him. The mysterious boy Krishna thus seems worth destroying simply because he is an unknown quantity. Krishna is growing ever more popular as he repeatedly aids the herders, and Kamsa suspects he may soon become a political rival. Kamsa cannot see that his own actions have led his subjects to seek Krishna's aid.

Kamsa never does learn. At the end of his life, reeling under Krishna's final assault, Kamsa literally doesn't know what has hit him. Dragged by the hair down to his death, he cannot see his assailant and would not recognize him if he could. Warned that the supreme god who had killed him in a previous life might do so again, Kamsa had boasted, "Not even Indra scares me!" Kamsa does not know which god to fear most. Vishnu is entirely beyond his ken.

Throughout most of his youth Krishna is kept busy responding to Kamsa's maneuvers. The story of how Krishna dispenses one by one with the demons sent against him until Kamsa himself is reached gives the narrative its basic structure. But right in the middle an incident occurs that seems unconnected. As the herders prepare to celebrate their favorite annual festival, honoring the rain god Indra, Krishna calls on them to worship instead the nearby Govardhana Hill. When Indra angrily sends a storm to punish them for acting as Krishna suggests, Krishna lifts up the Govardhana Hill to ward off Indra's torrents. In thus defying Indra, Krishna is not removing a clear threat to human well-being. In fact, Krishna's defiance of Indra is the only confrontation young Krishna enters into that is not prompted by some immediate human need. Tempting Indra's wrath seems to make no practical sense and indeed provokes disastrous consequences.

Krishna acknowledges that nothing is wrong with the logic of the old herder whom Krishna presses for an explanation of Indra's festival. Nonetheless, Krishna proposes that the herders give up this admittedly valuable custom to gain something better. Krishna is attempting here to point out the goal that lies beyond the successful outcome of his struggles with Kamsa. By lifting Govardhana, Krishna offers a positive vision of a better life worth striving for after all such obstacles have been swept away.

Indra is a heavenly symbol of earthly royalty. Kings on earth encourage public worship of the cloud-commanding Indra, king of heaven, because he dignifies their own occupation. By defying Indra, Krishna wishes to show the herders that, though all kings are not as bad as Kamsa, there is a limit to what should be expected of any king and consequently to the reverence due him.

Krishna urges the herders not to honor kings above that which contributes much more directly to their well-being, such as the neighboring Govardhana Hill and the cows who graze there. After all, with Indra's rains alone, human beings would be scarcely better off than without them. As do earthly kings, Indra enjoys performing his necessary function with a certain willfulness. At the outset of Indra's rainy season, a rapid shift typically occurs, from blasting heat that pulverizes the land to powder, to drenching, continuous rain. The rains uproot fences and make rivers and dry land an unbounded mucky chaos. Only Indra's deluge seems powerful enough to overcome the scorching sun of the dry season. Indra's chaos soon stirs with new life. Flooding fields and uprooting trees, the new rains also bring loam to enrich worn-out fields. Before long these same swirling waters will nourish crops to tide over the harsh seasons ahead. So despite his willfulness, Indra is welcomed when he roars in to launch his monsoon torrents astride his cloud-elephant Airavata, with an entire herd of cloud-elephants thundering behind.

As king of the skies, Indra rides a white, four-tusked elephant, just as kings on earth ride their gray, two-tusked elephants. Indians seem to have always associated kings with elephants. Like kings, elephants are powerful and thus useful but hard to control. Elephants, moreover, become especially hard to control when seized by a mysterious annual frenzy that bears a startling resemblance to Indra's annual monsoon onslaught. For several weeks a year elephants may race restlessly about, bellowing until the earth trembles. At these times they rain down a pungent, oily fluid from glands located between their eyes and ears (see illustration, page 14). In Sanskrit, this fluid is called *mada*, cognate with the English *mad* (in Persian, *mast*). Under the influence of *mada* an elephant may assault anyone in sight. As the seizure advances the elephant's temples swell. If the flow of *mada* becomes a steady stream, it will trickle down into the elephant's mouth and arouse even greater fury.

Many elephants, on the other hand, never exude *mada*. Nor is it found in the young or the old. *Mada* does not begin to flow strongly until about the age of thirty, ten years after an elephant attains puberty, and disappears after the age of about forty-five. The rarity of *mada* and its association with prime health and the prime of life helped convince Indians that this was truly a royal frenzy.

Why do elephants secrete *mada*? Even today, no one is sure what its precise physical function is. Modern science has made no advance over an ancient Sanskrit compendium of elephant lore, the *Matanga-lila*, which lists the "eight excellences" of *mada* in elephants: "Excitement, swiftness, odor, love passion, complete florescence of the body, wrath, prowess, and fearlessness." According to the

Detail of figure 17. Indra's Elephant Airavata, with Mada
Flowing from His Temple to His Mouth

Matanga-lila, elephants were once timorous. So the god Brahma created *mada,* allocating half of it to elephants while dispersing the other half throughout the rest of the created universe. Thus elephants are said to have half of the world's *mada,* but there is a bit of it in everything else alive. "Trees reach their seasonal growth at the sight of *mada,* and other living things too are filled with joy at the thought of *mada.*" (Franklin Edgerton, *The Elephant Lore of the Hindus* [New Haven: Yale University Press, 1931], pp. 34, 80-81.) When elephants feel their special "excess of joy" and begin racing raucously about releasing *mada* from their temples, all the world experiences a thrill. It is scarcely surprising that Indians associate this typically annual *mada* frenzy of elephants with the annual monsoon onslaught of Indra's thunderclouds. The rainy season seems to happen because once a year Indra and his cloud-elephants go mad and in a wild drunken state give new energy to the world.

The seventeenth-century image of Airavata reproduced above depicts a moon painted over the elephant's *mada* gland. Even today, Indian trainers decorate their elephants in this fashion because the milk-white moon is also associated in Indian mythology with the return to earth of moisture and life robbed by the sun. Like *mada,* the "liquid" moon is believed to be in some sense linked to the sap of plants. Indeed, all the world's liquids are believed by the *Harivamsa*'s poet to be interconnected in a great circle. For example, in a story referred to in the *Harivamsa* that describes the churning of the ocean (see figure 21, page 74), the sap of the plants growing on the mountain that is used as a churning stick merges with the ocean's salt water to form milk. When churned further the milk produces the *amarta*, nectar of immortality, which the gods drink to stay alive but which in turn causes drunkenness leading to Indra's stormy rampage, which fills the rivers that water the earth as they flow to the ocean. If all earthly life were to cease, the world's diverse liquids would drain down into an undivided sea on which Vishnu would lie asleep. To prevent this, they must be periodically impelled forward. The churning of the ocean, like the elephant's *mada* seizure and Indra's furious torrent, is seen as an impetus necessary to keep the world's vital juices flowing from creature to creature, from sphere to sphere.

The forceful contribution to the sustaining of life made so self-importantly by Indra and his cloud-elephants each year stirs up new energies. But this alone, in the *Harivamsa*'s view, would not be enough. Mad Indra can and does arouse, but it is Krishna who makes fulfillment possible. For fulfillment a different mood is needed, a mood that is delicate, delightful, restrained. A tree does not attain fulfillment simply because its sap rises; it must also produce a flower to receive pollen. Human beings, similarly, cannot flourish by lust alone. Human sexual fulfillment must be beautiful, an exquisite communion, as tender as a bee's visit to a flower.

Insuring that all the energy Indra stirs up is made beneficial requires skills that are gentler and steadier than any Indra possesses. These are skills which Krishna preeminently exemplifies when he lifts the Govardhana Hill and transforms Indra's angry torrent into a calm flow of life-giving water. But in entering into a showdown with Indra, Krishna is not simply seeking to raise himself above Indra. He is also seeking to raise up the herders with him, because the herders possess many of these same quieter skills. Krishna urges that the herders honor the Govardhana Hill because in doing so they will be honoring themselves and their own contribution as cowherds to the world's welfare.

The word *Go-vardhana* means ''cow-benefiting,'' and for the herders to worship their nearby cow-benefiting hill is thus at the same time to worship their own herds and, more generally, the cow itself. In the universe as a whole, Krishna suggests, the cow symbolizes best those aspects of the natural order that are wholly benign. And just as kings have a temperamental affinity to elephants, so are herders associated in a sympathetic bond with their cows. Kings and elephants are mixed blessings at best, while the cow and cowherds exemplify a deeper, gentler principle in nature.

The relative worth of kings and cowherds is the theme of a brief tale told in the *Harivamsa* before the story of Krishna is begun:

> *Eager to help his people, King Parthu seized his bow and arrows and decided to slay Earth. The frightened Earth transformed herself into a cow and ran away. Parthu chased after her, determined to destroy her. Earth fled through the skies, terrified by the sight of Parthu brandishing his bow and his blazing, sharp arrows. Parthu was strong, disciplined, sinless, glowing with energy, one whom even the immortals would find difficult to withstand. Seeing that she could not escape, Earth bowed and said, "Parthu, don't you know it would be wrong to kill a female? How can you support your subjects without me? Instead of killing me, you should spare me for, living, I can give your subjects much more food. Females, they say, should not be slain by those born of females. Great King, do not abandon justice."*
>
> *Hearing these words, the wise king stayed his hand and said to Earth, "It would certainly be sinful for one person to kill many for no good reason. But when killing can increase the happiness of many, it is no great sin, not even a minor sin. If I kill you, it would be to feed my people. You must die if you cannot do something at once to appease their hunger. You say you can sustain my people. Do so and you may be my daughter and gain my protection. If you can, dispel this dreadful famine which made me determine to kill you."*
>
> *Earth replied, "Lord, all this I shall certainly accomplish. See this calf of mine, on whom I dote. If you spare me, I shall let my milk flow with equal love for others everywhere."*

The story then relates that King Parthu milked the earth-cow, bringing forth in addition to milk "all the kinds of grains by which people live even today."

The earth in this tale is personified as a cow fleeing through the heavens. In the story of Krishna lifting Govardhana, the herders' own cows and the Govardhana Hill become symbols of the life-sustaining earth. Close at hand, they represent in ways which every herder can see that the earth's natural order is benign

1. The Earth-Cow Flees King Parthu

but also vulnerable. Given a chance, the earth-cow will produce nourishing food, but if shortsightedly abused, she will die. By lifting up the Govardhana Hill, Krishna shelters the earth-cow from Indra's devastating rains, but what Krishna does so dramatically is no different from what the herders do in their more modest ways in caring for their cows every day. Krishna wants the herders to have a higher estimation of themselves. Honoring an earthly king is like honoring the god of rain: not evil, but something to be done with a sense of proportion. That sense of proportion will come spontaneously when one realizes that one's own role as a human caretaker of life is even more important than the king's special role, and that one's power as a vessel containing a spark of cosmic force is sufficient to stand up to anything kings or the elements can generate. With Vishnu's help, human herders can keep the earth-cow alive, and with adequate care, the earth-cow will sustain human life.

The lesson of Govardhana is a distillation of the lesson of Krishna's life as a whole. The story of Krishna demonstrates in a heightened way what all human beings are capable of. Krishna shows that a human being, a two-armed, flesh-and-blood mortal, when energized by the spirit of the highest god Vishnu, can stand up to myriads of multi-armed gods and demons. Every human herder has a small spark of Vishnu's energy within. Every human being can perform miracles by letting Vishnu's energy express itself in his or her life. Even the humble Govardhana Hill, with Vishnu's support, can withstand all Indra's might.

THE STORY

Whoever shall recount this wondrous tale
Will never know misfortune or taste grief.

Harivamsa, 113.82

2. *Brahma, Shiva, Indra, a Herder and the Earth-Cow*
Ask the Unseen Vishnu to Manifest Himself on Earth

❀{ I }❀

Birth

THE city of Mathura was shaped like a crescent moon. It was bordered by the Yamuna River on one side and encircled on the other by a moat. Stoutly barred gates formed the only entrances. But within Mathura's walls could be seen graceful towers and pleasant parks. In the busy streets, cheerful people were coming and going. Many were vigorous men skilled in fighting. Elephants, horses, and chariots also abounded. The city, moreover, contained multitudes of splendid jewels, because Mathura was the capital of a populous and wealthy country. The fields around Mathura always produced rich and savory crops, because Indra the rain god brought showers in the proper season. This fine city brimming with happy men and women was governed in these fortunate days by the virtuous heir of a valorous line, King Ugrasena.

But the son of King Ugrasena was the vicious Kamsa. Large-eyed, like a lion in strength, in his previous life as a sky-roaming demon he had been slain in battle by Vishnu. Reborn as the son of Ugrasena's queen, Kamsa when he grew up seized the throne from his father and began provoking great terror among other rulers of the earth, indeed among all creatures. His arrogance and cruelty made people's hair stand on end. He always took the wrong path, disregarding every kingly duty. Disliking his own subjects, he took pleasure in abusing them.

Many other demons had been slain by Vishnu along with the demon who was reborn as Kamsa, and they too now came to earth to aid Kamsa's designs. The horse demon Hayagriva was born as the horse Keshin and began terrorizing Vraja, an area near Mathura. Vile, shrill-braying, this ill-tempered horse became an eater of human flesh. The demon Arishta, who could change his shape at will, became a big-humped bull who menaced cows. The haughty wind demon Pralamba took up residence close by the Bhandira fig tree in Vrindavana, a region of Vraja. And the ass demon Dhenuka seized a grove of palmyra trees there and frightened everyone away. Two other demons, originally shaped like a boar and a colt, were transformed into professional wrestlers who worked for King Kamsa.

Fleeing from the skies, this plague of demons led by Kamsa had begun ravaging the country. So Vishnu, at the request of the other gods, decided to come to earth in human form to restore justice. But before Vishnu reached the earth, a powerful skyborne ascetic named Narada who was familiar with the gods' intentions descended from the heavens and headed for Mathura. He stopped to rest in a garden near the city and sent a messenger to announce his coming to the king. When told of his arrival, Kamsa came out quickly, for he knew the reputation of the sinless Narada, prince of visionaries. The king bowed down humbly before the sage, whose body glowed with energy. Kamsa then offered him a jeweled throne, gleaming like fire, on which the proud Narada calmly took his seat. He told Kamsa, "Great King, you have received me in a very respectful manner. So now listen to what I shall say.

"As you know, I often travel to the heavenly paradise located high atop Mount Meru near the sun. I have seen Chitraratha's garden there and bathed in the pure streams flowing through it. I have seen the holy Ganges as it courses through the heavens before descending to earth, and I have purified myself at one after another of its divine bathing places. I have heard Brahma's heavenly musicians play while Brahma listened, surrounded by his attendant gods with their white turbans, all seated on splendid thrones brilliant with various jewels. I have myself played the *vina* in Brahma's court. This is how I know, Kamsa, that the gods are forming schemes against you. These schemes involve Devaki, your aunt, the sister of your father, Ugrasena. Kamsa, her eighth child will kill you. He who is the highest of the gods, higher even than those of Brahma's court, supreme in the three heavens: this god will destroy you. His identity is the gods' greatest secret. I will not name him. But you have encountered him before, since he destroyed you also in your former life. Kamsa, your best hope is to try to slay him at birth. Because I was pleased by the courtesies you showed me, I have told you this. I wish you well. But now I must leave."

Kamsa brooded a long time after Narada had left. Then, laughing loudly, his teeth glittering, he told his attendants, "Narada isn't so clever as he thinks. I will never be intimidated by any of these gods, even if they are led by Indra. I don't care whether they attack me when I am ready or asleep, when I am set for battle or drunk. With my two great arms I could shake the earth. Who is there in all the world strong enough to shake me? I am first among all the world's

3. Narada, His Vina *Resting on His Shoulder, is Received with Honor*

creatures —human beings, birds, and beasts. I could destroy them all if I chose! I have demons under my control, like the horse Keshin, and Pralamba and Dhenuka; like Arishta the bull and Putana and Kaliya. They can take any form I wish and roam every land to strike down those who cross me. I even know people's innermost thoughts. Anyone who pleases me and seeks my aid has nothing to fear. And this Narada says I might be killed by a child! Narada is surely bent on destroying my happiness. He has a meddlesome mind. He loves to wander about making trouble." All the way back to the palace, Kamsa kept prattling away boastfully like this. His thoughts were wild and angry.

When he reached his private apartments, Kamsa called together his closest advisers. "Narada says," he informed them, "that a threat to me could spring from the womb of my aunt, Devaki. You must help me kill her children. Devaki will be confined to her rooms, and though permitted to conceive, she will be very carefully watched when she is with child. I shall instruct my women to count the months from conception so we may know when she is to give birth. Devaki's husband, Vasudeva, will be confined too and closely watched by dependable eunuchs. But neither my women nor my eunuchs must explain the reasons for these measures. These are the kinds of ploys human-beings must use to gain their ends, though spells and potions can also sometimes veer fate around.''

Kamsa had thus begun conferring with his advisers about how to deal with the threat of which Narada had warned him. As he listened quietly from the heavens to Kamsa giving these cruel commands, Vishnu mused, ''Seven children must die at Kamsa's hands because I am not to be born until Devaki has conceived eight times.'' Pondering this dilemma, Vishnu recalled to mind the six embryos who floated in a watery womb below the earth. They had once been mighty demons and, in fact, were sons of Kamsa himself in his earlier incarnation as the demon Kalanemi. At one time, these six demons, their hair wild and matted, had inflicted severe austerities on themselves. Disregarding their own forebears, they dedicated their efforts instead to the god Brahma. At long last Brahma was gratified and granted each of them a boon. The six demons then all said, ''If we have indeed pleased you, let us never be slain by any god or man.'' ''So be it,'' Brahma had replied, and had returned to the heavens. But Hiranyakashipu, grandfather of Kalanemi and thus great-grandfather of the six youths, said angrily, ''Since you have forgotten me in your prayers, I condemn you to be killed by someone who is neither god nor man but a demon—your own father. My curse is for you to live henceforth as sleeping embryos until the time comes for you to be placed in Devaki's womb, when you will be killed by your father Kalanemi in his human form as Kamsa.''

Remembering all this, Vishnu came down to where the six embryos were resting in the care of Nidra, goddess of sleep. Vishnu said to her, ''Take these six embryos one by one to Devaki. Place one in her womb each time she conceives. They will die, and in this way Kamsa will be tricked. Devaki's seventh child will be Balarama, light-colored as the moon. He will be magically removed from

Devaki's womb in the seventh month and transferred to the womb of Rohini, Vasudeva's other wife. Devaki will be said to have miscarried, and, as Rohini's child, Balarama will be spared. Then, Nidra, your turn will have come.

"I shall be the eighth child conceived by Devaki. At the very moment of my conception, you will enter the womb of Yasoda, wife of the cowherd Nanda. You will be born on the ninth day of the waning moon's cycle when the night is no longer young, at the dead of night under the star Vega in the constellation Lyra. I will be born then too, eight months after conception. Then I shall be transferred to Yasoda's side, you to Devaki. In this way Kamsa shall be deluded. Seizing your feet, he will dash you against a rock. But instead of being killed, you will rise into the sky to a place of eternal glory. In the heavens, your body will appear dark like mine, and your face bright like Balarama's. You will have four sturdy long arms. In your four hands you will hold a trident, a golden sword, a pot filled with honey, and a flawless lotus. You will wear dark blue linen, with a yellow shawl. On your breasts a necklace of pearls will shimmer like moonbeams. Highlighted by starry earrings, your face will rival the moon in lustre. A triple diadem will gleam in your hair. Your arms strong as staves will be twined about by hissing snakes. Peacock plumes will be atop your standard, peacock feathers will adorn your arms and ankles. Fierce creatures will attend you. Indra will anoint you, take you as his sister, and give you a place high in the Vindhya hills. Vowed to virginity, you will stride through the three worlds slaying demons and pursuing righteousness. You shall grant favors to those who please you and assume different guises at will. Because your creatures will always hunger for sacrificial flesh, animal offerings will be made in your name on the ninth day of the waning moon's cycle. People who honor you and know my power will never want anything, whether sons or riches. Men will pray to you when lost in desolate forests or drowning at sea or accosted by robbers. You will embody Success, Prosperity, Courage, Fame, Modesty, Learning, Restraint, Intelligence, Evening, Night, Brightness, Sleep, Death. You will comfort those who seek your aid when they fear arrest or torture, the death of a son, the loss of wealth, or their own disease or death. Once you have tricked Kamsa, you alone will enjoy the world. With your triumph over Kamsa, my influence shall again prevail on earth."

When Vishnu had given her these instructions, he vanished. "So be it," Nidra said, bowing, and set forth.

Devaki then conceived seven times. As each of her first six children came from her womb, Kamsa seized the child and dashed it to death against a rock. But Devaki's seventh child was transferred to Vasudeva's other wife, Rohini, by a ploy of Nidra. One night Rohini fell to the ground, overpowered by the deluding Nidra. As in a dream, Rohini saw a child coming out of her womb. Believing that she had miscarried, she became distraught. But Nidra said to her, "You are destined to bear a son." Covering her face to hide her joy, Rohini then returned to her own rooms bearing Devaki's child. Kamsa was told that Rohini's dead child was Devaki's seventh son.

When Devaki conceived an eighth time, she was watched with even greater care because this time the child was to be the one warned of by Narada. In a small herder encampment in Vraja, Yasoda conceived a child at the same time as Devaki. Yasoda's womb was entered by Nidra, Vishnu's daughter, as Devaki's womb was entered by Vishnu. Both women gave birth at the same moment, before their full term in the eighth month. Yasoda, wife of the cowherd Nanda, gave birth to a girl; to Devaki, Krishna was born.

At that splendid midnight moment, the oceans and the earth trembled. Fires that had died down flared up. Gentle winds blew, the hazy clouds lifted, and stars could be seen brightly shining in celebration of Krishna's birth. For the inexpressible Krishna had dumbfounded all the universe with his beauty. Indra's long-silent thunder-drums rolled, and flowers rained down from the sky. Sages, nymphs, and celestial musicians approached, praising Krishna with words and auspicious sounds.

Vasudeva picked up his glorious son and with divine assistance went out of their barred quarters, coming finally to where Nanda and Yasoda were camped nearby. Without their knowledge, Vasudeva substituted one newborn infant for the other. Vasudeva then returned the way he had come and placed Yasoda's infant daughter beside Devaki. Once the exchange of the two babies had been accomplished, Vasudeva, still quaking with terror, went to inform the king of the birth of a light-complexioned daughter. Hearing this news, Kamsa rushed out with his bodyguards and went straight to Devaki's room. "Where is the child?" he demanded. "Hand her over!" The women attending Devaki began to wail. Devaki said, "My lord, I have given birth to a sweet daughter. You have killed my fine sons. This little one too is as good as dead. See for yourself if you like." The deluded Kamsa rejoiced, thinking she was stillborn. The little baby with hair

4. Devaki and Vasudeva Worship the Newborn Krishna Represented as Vishnu

still wet from the womb did seem nearly lifeless as she was placed at the king's feet. Kamsa's servant nonetheless seized her determinedly by the leg, lifted her up high, and dashed her against a rock in the courtyard. But instead of being crushed to death, she sprang into the sky transformed into a goddess adorned with garlands and pastes. She was four-armed and garbed in blue and yellow robes. Her hips were wide as a cart. Her breasts, round as an elephant's temples, were heavy as rainclouds. Her face was like the moon, bright as lightning in color, her eyes brilliant as the morning sun. Dancing, laughing, her voice like thunder, glowing with defiance, savagely quaffing strong liquors, she moved through the night sky attended by dark and frightening beasts. Laughing aloud, she said fiercely,

27

5. Leaving Krishna with Yasoda, Vasudeva Returns to the Palace Carrying Nidra

"Kamsa, you dashed me against a rock. So when your murderer crushes you, I shall claw your body and drink your blood." Then she rose with her attendants high into the heavens.

Kamsa was stricken with terror for his life. Fearful and ashamed, he returned to Devaki's side and asked to speak to her alone. Plaintively he admitted, "I killed all your children, even though you are my father's sister, because one of your children was predicted to become my murderer. But now this goddess taunts me, saying my murderer is thriving somewhere else. Because I was desperate, I killed members of my own family, but still it seems I could not change fate. It was futile to resist. All the same, you should not grieve for your children, Devaki. If I had not ended their lives, Death would have. Death is the only real enemy we have, since Death is ahead for us all. Do not waste away from grief, lamenting your lost babies. Death is ordained for every creature. I fall at your feet like a son, Devaki. Don't be angry with me. I know I have done you injury."

Tears streaked her drawn face as Devaki gazed down at the humbled king. "Rise, my son," she said gently. "I know you are not the reason my children died. These killings were done by you only in appearance. The true reality is concealed from us. Even if a person is not murdered in infancy or childhood or youth, Death is never averted. For the unborn no less than for those of us who are born, there can be no foreknowledge. Even the unborn go how and where they are led. My son, do not think that you have taken my babies from me. Their deaths were foreordained. In truth, even birth occurs as part of a previsioned plan and not because of the actions of men and women."

Soothed by Devaki's words, Kamsa returned to his own chambers. Still restive, he was penitent but not tranquil.

Vasudeva had meanwhile secretly returned to Nanda's camp. The year before, Vasudeva had arranged for Rohini to take refuge with Nanda in Vraja, where she had given birth to Balarama, whose face was more splendid than the moon. Using his concern for Balarama as a pretext for coming, Vasudeva spoke guardedly to Nanda. "I beg you to go back to Vraja quickly," he said, "and take Yasoda and your newborn son away from this place. Perform the birth rites for both boys, my son and yours. Do everything necessary to insure their well-being. Care for them attentively so that they may grow up happily together in Vraja.

"I shall never see my dear son Balarama's face. But this is the only way to save him. Only if he is raised apart from me will I be able to continue the line of my ancestors. Lacking the power to oppose Kamsa, I am forced to use deception. Balarama, you see, would not have been safe here from Kamsa's wrath. Nanda, please look upon my only son Balarama and this dear son of yours with equal love. Guide them carefully past the difficulties all children face, and keep them safe from any demons. I must warn you, whatever you do, never pasture your herds in Vrindavana. That is where Keshin lives, who destroys cows and men. Beware too of injury from snakes and insects and vultures. And in the stableyard children may be accidentally injured even by a cow or a calf. Nanda, the night is over. Birds are singing, hinting of the dawn, urging you to go quickly."

Responding to Vasudeva's desire, Nanda and Yasoda made preparations for the trip home. Nanda placed the sleeping Krishna in a strong sling secured across his shoulders. To avoid detection, they traveled back toward Vraja by a little-used, winding footpath hugging the Yamuna's shore.

Soon Nanda and Yasoda with the infant Krishna safely reached Vraja. Verged by deep woods and cooled by breezes from the Yamuna River, this luxuriant district had at its center the Govardhana Hill. Everything here seemed graceful and charming. Cows were nursing their calves or grazing in sweet-smelling, carefully tended groves free of brambles where fierce beasts might hide. The cows ambled about easily, entering and leaving ponds and reservoirs by graded paths. Bulls scratched their shoulders and rubbed their horns against big trees. In the distance the ground was strewn with fallen forest trees, and hungry hawks, jackals, and lions cried out in their desire for prey. But nearby the trees were hung with luscious fruit and flowers. Many carts were going freely to and fro, and the woods resounded with the varied calls of songbirds. Within the camp could be heard the happy sounds of cows lowing, answered by their calves. Here cows and calves were tethered to posts by ropes or fenced in by thorny hedges. Cow dung was scattered plentifully about.

From home to home the sounds of churning filled the air. The women of the camp were churning so vigorously that buttermilk overflowed, making the ground moist. The breezes were nicely scented by the butter used in cooking. Small boys with tousled hair scampered about. Young women wearing blue and yellow breast cloths and with their ears adorned with wildflowers were returning from the river bearing jars of water on their heads.

Nanda was delighted by all these familiar sights and smells. Seeing him, the herders raised a welcoming shout. Old men and women rushed out to greet him. Arriving at length at his own compound, Nanda was welcomed there by Rohini.

The sun-like baby Krishna, Vishnu come to earth, was thus brought to the herder camp without being recognized and was accepted there simply as the child of Nanda and Yasoda.

6. *Herder Women Admire the Baby Krishna*

❖ II ❖

Infancy

K RISHNA enjoyed a happy infancy among the herders of Vraja. He was aptly named, for *krishna* means "dark," and the small body into which the immortal Vishnu had entered was dark as an ocean stormcloud.

Once when Krishna was still very small, his doting mother, Yasoda, left him sleeping soundly under a cart while she went to the river. In her absence, Krishna awoke and began to chortle and stretch his arms and legs. Before long he over-turned the cart under which he had been placed with one kick of his tiny foot and crawled away crying for his mother's breast. Yasoda now was returning from the river with as much eagerness as a cow to her calf. Milk welled up in her breasts as she hurried back to her dear child. But when she saw the cart toppled, and the jugs and jars it had held broken and scattered about, she cried out in horror and snatched up her child. She could not understand how the cart had been up-ended. She knew there had been no windstorm. Frightened, she murmured, "My darling, what will your father say? He will be angry when he learns I left you sleeping under a cart that fell over. Why did I go to bathe in the river just then? Only my foolishness exposed you to this danger."

Dressed in reddish-orange clothes, Nanda had been spending the day follow-ing his grazing herds. When he returned, he too saw the toppled cart by the door, its wheels scattered about, its yoke cast off. Nanda rushed inside, his eyes filling with tears. "Is my son safe?" he cried out. Seeing Krishna nursing peacefully at his mother's breast, he asked anxiously, "My beloved, was there a fight between two bulls?"

"I don't know," Yasoda stammered tearfully. "I went to the river to wash my clothes and when I came back the cart was lying broken on the ground." Several boys who heard them talking said, "Your baby did it with his foot. We saw it."

33

"That is astonishing," said everyone who heard the boys' story. Their eyes wide with wonder, the herders set the cart upright and put its wheels back on.

Another time, King Kamsa's ally, the demon wet nurse Putana, came to the camp in the middle of the night while the people there were asleep. Roaring like a tiger but with the form of a vulture, she alighted on the cart beside which Krishna was resting. Putana offered the little baby her poison-heavy breast, and Krishna sucked and sucked until he had ripped off her breast. He sucked away her very life and then began to cry. The whole neighborhood awoke with a start. The herders found Putana lying senseless on the ground with one breast gone as if ripped off by lightning. They stood around her wondering, "What's this? Who has killed her?" When everyone had finally gone bewildered back to bed, Nanda confided to Yasoda, "I don't understand what is going on. But I am fearful some harm may come to our son."

"I don't understand it either," murmured Yasoda. "I was sleeping soundly until I was awakened by our son's cries." Though he said nothing of it to Yasoda, Nanda and his relations were fearful that Kamsa might be behind what had happened.

Before long Krishna had grown to be as vigorous and sturdy as his older brother. Pale-skinned, moon-like Balarama and the darker, sun-like Krishna did everything together. They slept on the same bed, ate the same foods, wore each other's clothes, played the same games. In their play Krishna and Balarama were as intimately linked by mutual glances as the sun and moon by their rays. For the two brothers were both incarnations of Vishnu. The spirit that animates the whole universe had entered the world of human beings in the guise of two little boys living in a cowherd camp.

They loved to crawl about everywhere and squirm in the dust like snakes or bold little elephants. Sometimes they became so besmeared with ashes and cow dung that they resembled holy men. At other times they would crawl right in with the calves in their stalls and end up covered with dung from head to toe.

7. *Putana is Drained of Life*

These antics delighted their father, even when others now and then became annoyed. Large-eyed, with tousled dark hair framing their glowing faces, their beauty was exquisite.

Each day they seemed livelier and more determined than ever to crawl out of sight and scamper off around the camp. Nanda would do nothing about it. But one day Yasoda became so annoyed that she took the lotus-eyed Krishna out into the courtyard, scolded him soundly, and tied him by a rope round his waist to a heavy wooden mortar used for husking grain. "Crawl away *now* if you like!" she announced triumphantly and returned to her housework.

As soon as her back was turned, Krishna crawled out of the courtyard and across the fields, dragging the heavy mortar behind him. Before long he passed between two closely spaced trees, which held back the mortar. But the baby Krishna kept right on going, pulling the mortar behind him, until he had toppled those two ancient trees. None of the herders saw the mysterious infant manifest his divine energy in this way. But some minutes later, several women going to the river found the little child playing and laughing among the broken branches of the fallen trees. Terrified and weeping, they rushed to Yasoda, crying, "Come quick, Yasoda. You mustn't wait. Those two wishing trees have fallen right on top of your baby. He is tied fast round the waist by a rope like a calf and is gurgling away as if nothing had happened. Get up! Be quick! You think you're so clever, you foolish woman, and now because of your carelessness your son has barely escaped death."

Yasoda hurried off crying with horror toward the two uprooted trees. She saw her tiny son between them, still firmly tied to the mortar by the rope round his waist. All the herders were soon crowding round to see this amazing sight. They argued among themselves, asking why the two tallest trees in the whole camp had fallen when there had been no wind or rain, no thunderbolt and no infuriated elephant. "This is a calamity," they all agreed. "Those trees were a great blessing to the camp. Now they are as useless as spent clouds. But even in falling down they have been good to you, Nanda, for they did not harm your little son."

"This is the third strange thing to happen in this camp," someone pointed out. "That cart overturned. Then a vulture fell down dead. And now these trees have fallen over. I think we shouldn't graze our cows here any longer. If we stay, something else is sure to happen."

8. *Yasoda Ponders a Strange Occurrence*

Nanda quickly ripped loose his little son from the heavy mortar, and placing him on his lap, gazed at him as if he were a long-dead person who had returned to life. Then they all went home. Nanda scolded Yasoda. Because of this the herder girls sometimes called Krishna *Damodara*, which means "Rope-Sashed."

These are the amazing things Krishna did while still a baby living among the herders of Vraja.

❖⟪ III ⟫❖

Childhood

BY the time Krishna and Balarama were seven and eight, they were old enough to have some responsibility for herding. Krishna wearing yellow clothes, Balarama in blue, they raced cheerfully about after the calves in their charge. They fashioned bracelets from peacock feathers and daubed themselves with yellow and white pastes. Shining locks of black hair framed their faces. Crowned with leaves and lotuses, draped with wildflower garlands, they resembled budding young trees. Their ropes slung across their chests like priestly threads, they whiled away idle hours playing reed flutes and stringed instruments made from gourds. Sometimes they would play together, at other times they fell sound asleep side by side on a bed of leaves. Enjoying themselves thoroughly, they cavorted through the fields after their calves like two lustrous colts.

But one day Krishna said to Balarama, "I don't think we should graze our calves here any more. The grass is gone, shrubs are scarce, and many of the trees have been cut down. What used to be a rich woodland is now as bare as the sky. Even our fine stableyard trees have been turned into firewood. We used to graze our calves near the village. Now we must travel a long way to find grass. The trees were once full of birds. Now they have flown off, and it is much too quiet. With no birds to sing for us, no gentle breezes to cool us, there is no enjoyment. Staying on here is like eating tasteless food. Firewood and fruit are so scarce, they are being bought and sold, just as in a city. A thriving herder camp is the glory of the hill regions, and the glory of a herder camp is its woodlands. How can herders live in a place where there is no grass? We should find a home where our calves will have plenty to eat. Who wants to live behind barred doors like people who own farms and fine houses? The best lives are those lived by roaming herders and by migratory birds. When cows are cramped like this, their dung and urine begin fouling all the grass. The cows don't like it and their milk is soon not fit to drink. I think we should pack up and move.

38

"I have heard of a place called Vrindavana," Krishna continued. "It is also in Vraja, but it is nicely wooded and has good water and grass. They say it has many flowering Kadamba trees and plenty of fruit. There are no thorns or harmful insects. Cool breezes blow through the trees. It would be delightful at every season. The Govardhana Hill is near. And by Govardhana is the gigantic Bhandira fig tree, its high-spreading branches hanging like a rain cloud in the sky. The Yamuna River flows through the meadows. In Vrindavana we would have the Govardhana Hill, the Bhandira fig tree, and the Yamuna River. Surely it would be better to take our calves and cows there and leave this dismal place. But I suppose I must create a crisis before our people will move."

As Krishna pondered what to do, hundreds of voracious wolves sprang from the hairs of his body. Like Krishna, these wolves were dark-faced, and they bore on their bodies the mystical curl of hair visible on Krishna's own chest. The wolves dashed off and were soon spreading havoc in the camp. They moved in packs sometimes numbering five, sometimes ten, sometimes twenty or thirty or even a hundred. They devoured calves. Children were carried off in the night. The herders grew afraid to go out into the pastures to tend their cattle or across the river or into the woods to gather anything. The whole herder encampment was so frightened by the marauding wolves that no one would move from the spot.

Seeing the devastation increasing daily, the herder men and women came together to discuss what they should do. "We can't stay here," they all agreed. "We must find some other pastureland where our cows and all of us will be safe. Let's go right now. Let's take our herds and start out today before we are all killed by wolves. These wolves are terrible with their smoke-gray and reddish-brown bodies, fangs flashing in their dark muzzles, howling dreadfully through the night. 'My son has been carried off!' 'My brother!' 'My calf!' 'My cow!' —These are the shouts we hear every day."

Saddened by the women's weeping and the constant lowing of bereaved cows, the elders decided to move the camp. Knowing that their minds were made up, Nanda spoke out eloquently. "Today we have reached a decision," he said, his voice as resonant as that of Brihaspati, preceptor of the gods. "If we are to go, let us act quickly. Make ready without delay."

Others from the throng called out their agreement. "Let the carts be yoked, the herds of calves gathered and pots and pans loaded! Let's leave this place for Vrindavana!"

39

9. The Herders Move to Vrindavana

The whole camp was a tumult. Carts rumbled down every lane. The sound they made was like a tiger's roar or the deep voice of the sea. The line of women leaving the settlement filled the road as stars fill the sky. Carrying their churns, with pots perched on their heads, they wore breast cloths colored blue, yellow, and red. As they moved along the road, they were like the arc of a rainbow. The men with ropes slung from their bodies looked like trees hung with vines. With its waves of moving, gleaming carts, the procession was like the sea with its flying, wind-tossed waves. Almost in no time, the settlement had become a desert, swept clean of every object of value, filled only with crows looking for scraps.

Before long the slow procession reached Vrindavana, where shelters were quickly erected. Carts were scattered about the outskirts of the new encampment.

Within this circle the herders made fences for their cattle by interlacing the branches of thorny bushes. Everywhere the camp teemed with life. The ground was strewn with cart ropes used for yoking, and tethering ropes and churning ropes. Other ropes hung from hitching posts and churning sticks. Churns were being washed with water. Rush mats were being attached to ridgepoles made from newly felled trees. Cow stalls were being readied, and mortars for husking grain set in place. Fires were blazing with flames that pointed eastward as sacrificial butter was poured on them. Bedding was being laid down on leather ground coverings. Women moved about carrying water or dragging back branches that the men had cut with axes. Everyone rejoiced in Vrindavana's rich woodlands, charming groves, and rains sweet as nectar. The herders and their cows had found a home rivaling the garden of the gods. It was just as Krishna had described it.

Because there was sufficient grass even in the hot season, the herders' cows never became sickly. Krishna and Balarama once again took pleasure in leading their calves to pasture. The two brothers also enjoyed plunging into the Yamuna River to cool off.

And then the monsoon rains began, breaking the burning heat, giving plants new life, and kindling human hearts to love. Heavy black clouds rolled in, their bellies streaked with rainbows. The wind-whipped clouds covered the sun as rippling grass spread over the earth. The earth's surface became as supple and fresh as a young girl's skin. As the rains fell, the smoke and flames of forest fires were quelled, and in their stead red Sakragopa beetles flickered harmlessly through the woods. Orange Kadamba blooms and yellow banana flowers, bright against the dark clouds, also made the forest seem still on fire. But the mountains once scorched by flame were now capped by plumes of mist, not smoke. The waters had released the earth from fierce heat.

Kutaja flowers smiled alluringly. The scent of Kadamba blossoms, so delectable to bees, filled the woods. And with the countryside made so fresh and sweet-smelling, men and women began to tremble with pleasurable excitement. Big black bees hummed, frogs croaked. Maddened peacocks emitting shrill screams began their courting dance. Every creature seemed moved by one desire.

Soon the rains grew heavier. Streams ran full and fast and deep, carrying off trees along their banks. Birds, their feathers wet, huddled in trees for cover as though exhausted, making no effort to fly. The sun seemed to have been swallowed up as the waters kept tumbling and roaring down. Lightning split the

10. *The Herders Set up Camp in Vrindavana*

summits of the green-sloped hills, sending boulders crashing below. With landmarks uprooted and water spreading everywhere, it was difficult to find one's way. All the earth seemed covered by a single damp garment. Rain-filled lakes and ponds spilled over into the pastures. Wild elephants, their trunks lifted high echoing the sounds of thunder, seemed like a herd of clouds come to earth.

Gazing up at the clouds heaving down their burdens, Balarama said, "Krishna! Look at the clouds! They have stolen the color of your skin and carried it up to the sky. At this time of year you become hidden. Dark clouds veil the moon, making it as hard to see as you. In the monsoon darkness, the sky looks like a pond of blue-black lotuses with their petals spread wide. Here below, the earth is covered everywhere with new grass. With clouds gathered at its summit and streams flowing down its green sides, Govardhana is now truly what its name suggests, a hill that benefits cows. The hill with its leaping streams, the woods with their fruit, the fields with their crops could not be more glorious! Just look at our Vrindavana, Krishna!"

Balarama could not stop praising all he saw. "No moon is seen any more at night, and in daytime there is no sun. With showers for arrows, the rainbow for his bow, lightning glinting off his cloud-armor, the sky is like a warrior ready for battle. As love-exciting winds blow about the fragrance of flowers, travelers away from home are made frantic with desire to return to their loved ones. The water-filled clouds driven forward by the wind make the sky resemble a billowing ocean. The sky is as deep and murky as the ocean too, because layers of high-piled clouds are swirling up and down around the tops of hills and tall trees. Cool winds are raising up waves on the lakes and at the same time making the grasses in the fields tremble and roll. So you see, the sky looks like the earth and the lakes look like the land. Sky and earth are one great ocean of water and movement." Balarama was still exulting in this way as the two brothers meandered back to the camp to rejoin their friends.

One day during this delectable season the dark-skinned, lotus-eyed Krishna wandered off by himself, carrying the staff and ropes he used to control his calves. Black sidelocks framed his face, and on his breast could be seen the curl of hair that was his special mark, just as the face is for the moon. His armbands glinted as he strolled along, and his yellow garments shimmered, bright as a cloud at sunset. His breath was as fragrant as if emanating from a lotus. Bees were attracted to his glowing face as if it were a lotus. The garlands he wore, fashioned of red Arjuna and orange Kadamba flowers, glistened like stars in the sky. On his chest, a peacock's feather suspended on a string round his neck trembled with each gentle gust of wind. Dark as a blue-black cloud, bedecked with flowers and leaves of every hue, Krishna looked like the rainy season personified. As he roamed through the pastures, he sometimes sang or played his sweet-voiced flute for his own enjoyment or to please his calves. He romped all over the countryside like a bounding blue-black cloud, delighting in the colorful love-stirring woodland, which resounded with the calls of peacocks and the echoes of rumbling clouds. Along the grassy paths, banana trees bloomed and sent forth new shoots. The flowers everywhere breathed out their perfume as strongly as a young girl sighing with desire. Rambling in these strong-scented woods stirred by fresh breezes, Krishna was ecstatic with joy.

Another time Krishna, along with the other herder boys, ambled toward the Bhandira fig tree. With its crown of rich leaves covering half the sky, it loomed like a cloud moored to the ground. The wind seemed eager to caress its richly leaved, heavily fruited boughs. Birds of many hues fluttering through its dark and variegated foliage made it seem tinged by a rainbow. Under its branches, twining about its downward-growing roots, tender flowering creepers thrived. Towering high, it was like a beneficent overlord for all the other plants of that country. Krishna felt inclined to halt by this massive kindly tree, and the herder boys spent the day there with their calves. Some played in the woods, others sang songs. Krishna accompanied them by playing on his reed flute and stringed gourd. He felt as happy as he had formerly been as Vishnu in paradise.

Then they led their calves along the bank of the Yamuna until they came to a spot where the trees were gracefully adorned with vines. An easy descent led down to the river's sweet-tasting water, fast-moving in some places, quiet in others. The wind made curving waves and tossed up sprays of foam. And as the wind lifted up the waves, it bent down answering branches arched over the water. Everywhere wild geese, ducks, and cranes called excitedly. The waters teemed with fish and glowed with yellow lotuses.

11. The Herder Boys Enjoy the Rainy Season

At this season the flooding Yamuna blended with the countryside around to make a landscape resembling a woman's recumbent form. Small streams flowing out from the main current were her feet, while rounded sandbars heaved up like her hips. Lotuses seemed like tender body hair. A whirlpool was her navel, waves were her belly's soft folds. Ruddy geese perched on the curving shores were the nipples of her swelling breasts. Trails of foam raised by skidding geese formed her bright smile. Gleaming lilies peeping up through looping leaves were her lively eyes hidden under curving brows. A long pool rimmed with moss had become her forehead rimmed with delicate locks of hair. Slender streams were her arms, subtle curves her ears, adorned with ducks as earrings. An expanse of waving marsh grass made a golden robe of silk ornamented by the geese moving through it. A line of leaping fish glinted like a silver belt. The cries of cranes sounded like a woman's anklets. Crocodiles and fish streaked her surface like accents of bright paste. Turtles were her beauty marks.

Some of her pools were polluted by the drinking of savage animals. But from her pure wells, human beings took water like infants drawing nourishment from their mother's full breasts. Strolling along beside this luxuriant wife of the ocean, Krishna contributed his own radiance to the Yamuna's glorious abundance.

A little distance farther along, Krishna came upon the biggest pool of all. Even a god could scarcely have crossed it. This pool was as deep and blank as a motionless sea. Its surface burned with the brilliance of a brushfire. Its stagnant depths were impenetrable, like the sky when thick with clouds. It was difficult to walk along its shore, which was pitted by large snake holes. The air above was empty of birds. Fumes rose from the water like smoke from a putrid fire. Animals and fish avoided that pool. What man would drink from it, what priest dare use it for rituals? And this huge pool was very near where the herders now made their home!

Peering down, Krishna wondered, "Whose pool is this? I'll bet Kaliya, king of snakes, black as soot, has come here. Perhaps he is trying to hide from his old foe Garuda, king of birds. Kaliya must be the one defiling the Yamuna like this. From fear of him, this country is deserted. The woods around are nearly impassable, with the grass overgrown and the trees a snarl of dangling roots, vines, and branches. The shores of the pool are choked with underbrush and slimy with moss. Kaliya's sentinels no doubt are posted there to scare off anyone trying to come here. I must get rid of Kaliya so these waters will be pure and easy to approach. With that snake gone, we can come here at any season. The water and the woods nearby would be good and pleasing. This is just the kind of task for which I took on a herder's life. I will climb up into that Kadamba tree and dive in. Kaliya had better look out!"

Krishna tightened his loincloth and climbed to the top of the Kadamba tree, where he seemed like a dark cloud among its branches. Then with a shout the lotus-eyed boy leapt into the middle of that great pool. The serpent king rose up quickly out of the water, his eyes wild with rage that his calm lair had been

46

12. *Krishna Subdues the Serpent King Kaliya*

disturbed. His upper body coiled about in the air like massing clouds. His mouths were fiery, with tongues flicking, and his five hoods were spread wide. The entire pool was filled by his coils as bright as fire. The Yamuna ran backwards as if to escape the frightful flames issuing from his five mouths. Sighting the little boy brashly swimming about, Kaliya angrily breathed forth streams of smoke and flame, which instantly consumed great trees on the shore. It seemed as if Kaliya might destroy the world. Soon his sons, wives, and servants appeared, all boundlessly powerful snakes, all belching poisonous fire. They twined their coils about Krishna, pinning down his hands and feet and rendering him motionless as a mountain. Then they sprayed him with venom and bit into him with their sharp fangs.

47

Krishna's friends had meanwhile raced back to the camp, crying out in tear-choked voices, "Krishna has gone mad and jumped into that snake pool! He is being devoured! Go quick and tell Nanda his son is being dragged down to his death!" The news hit Nanda like a bolt of lightning. He rushed off trembling toward that dread pool, followed by Balarama and all the other herders, from young girls to old men. Arriving at the shore they all began to wail. Amazed and grief-stricken, some cried out, "Krishna!"; others, "What have you done?"; others, "Now we shall all die!" Some of the women cried to Yasoda, "We are done for! Look, the serpent has seized your son. He is bound by the serpent's coils and will be dragged down like an animal. Yasoda, why haven't you fainted? Your heart must be made of stone. Look at Nanda! He is so dazed he is standing dumbfounded at the water's edge, transfixed with grief at the sight. Look! She is going to enter that pool to save her son!"

"She is right!" others cried. "Let's follow her and die, if need be, trying to save Krishna. We will not go home without him. Where is the day without the sun? Where is the night without the moon? Where are cows without a bull? Where is Vrindavana without Krishna? Without Krishna we are like cows robbed of our calves. We will never return without him."

Hearing these lamentations, Balarama reacted quickly. Since Balarama and Krishna had both been created from portions of Vishnu's unchanging essence, they were identical in understanding. "Krishna! Great-armed Krishna!" he cried out. "You had better subdue that snake fast. Everyone here is weeping pitifully, thinking your plight is desperate, because with their human intellects they believe you too are merely human!"

Realizing that Balarama was right, Krishna calmly spread apart his arms and snapped the serpent's stranglehold. Then he planted his foot on the slippery coils and, grabbing hold of the snake's central head, he bent it down and leapt up onto the top of his wide-spreading hood. Perched there on that monster's head, Krishna began to dance about, his armbands glinting as he moved.

Pummeled on the head by Krishna's dancing feet, the snake king soon weakened and began to vomit blood. In a trembling voice he said, "Krishna, I was stupid to be angry with you. Now I am done for, my venom is gone. Spare my life and I and all my wives and relations will obey your command!"

"I shall certainly never let you live in the waters of the Yamuna," Krishna replied firmly. "Go then, you snake, with all your wives and relations, and live in the ocean if you like. But if you or your followers or your children are ever seen around here again in the river or on land, they shall be immediately killed by me. Leave, so these waters will be wholesome. If you return, that will be the end of you. You will be safe in the ocean now, because when the bird king Garuda sees my footprints on your head, he will not harm you." Then, as all the herders watched, that huge, vanquished serpent swam meekly out of the pool and down the river out of sight, bearing Krishna's footprints on his head.

Krishna jumped back up onto the shore, where he was greeted with wonder by the herders, who honored him by worshipfully walking around him. Thrilled with joy, the other herders told Nanda, "You are indeed fortunate to have such a son. From now on we will honor your son as our protector in misfortune and as our lord. He has saved us all, herders and cows alike. The waters of the Yamuna have been made good and pure everywhere. Our cows can approach the river safely at any point. Foolishly we never saw that Krishna is a mighty being. He has been living here unrecognized all this time, like an undetected fire."

Praising Krishna in this way, the awestruck herders returned to their cowsheds, feeling as joyous as immortals entering paradise.

After Krishna had subdued the serpent king in the pool of the Yamuna, Krishna and Balarama resumed tending their calves. One day, as they were wandering about with their calves, they came upon a large palmrya palm grove to the north of the Govardhana Hill. They were delighted by this shady grove and raced about happily, as spirited as two young bulls. The grass there was rich and level because the soil was black and moist and free of hard clods and stones. The towering, dark, segmented trunks of the palms, laden at the top with fruit and foliage, looked like upraised elephant trunks.

"See those nuts!" Krishna said. "Let's shake some down. They smell ripe and I'll bet they would taste like nectar." Balarama obligingly shook the trees to make the nuts fall.

But that tempting grove was a dangerous place because Dhenuka with a great herd of other wild asses lived there. The ass demon Dhenuka had made the grove deathly quiet by frightening away every man, bird, and beast. When he heard the telltale sound of palmyra nuts falling, Dhenuka became as mad as an aroused

13. *Balarama Destroys the Ass Demon Dhenuka*

elephant. Following the sound, he grew angrier by the minute as he bore down on the two boys. His mane tossed, his eyes were hard. He brayed shrilly, tearing at the earth with his hooves, thrashing his tail, baring his teeth, seeming like Death. Rushing at Balarama as he stood beneath the palms, Dhenuka tried to bite him. Then he turned around and with his hind legs kicked the unarmed Balarama. But Balarama grabbed his hind legs and tossed him to the top of the tree. Then Dhenuka fell back down to his death, bringing plenty of nuts along with him. Dhenuka's haunches, back, and neck were broken in many places. Seeing that Dhenuka had been killed by his fall, Balarama started tossing the other asses up into the palm tree. Strewn with the dead asses and with nuts scattered about, the ground resembled an early autumn sky covered with breaking clouds.

Once Dhenuka and his followers had been dispatched, this seemingly delightful spot became truly agreeable. Fear was driven from the empty wood, and cows could now graze there undisturbed. Soon all the herders were pasturing their cattle in the grove without worry. Having made their calves happy, the two courageous brothers assembled a bed of leaves and settled down for a rest.

Later, Krishna and Balarama left the palmyra grove and, in high spirits, set out in the direction of the Bhandira fig tree. As they strolled through the lush pastures with their thriving herds, they would hum or sing or call to their cows and calves by name. With ropes slung over their broad shoulders and garlands of wild flowers adorning their breasts, they looked themselves like handsome young bulls. Smeared with bright pastes and wearing equally colorful garments, the two brothers resembled two clouds, one dark, one silvery white, both ringed with rainbows. Wearing necklaces of leaves, with grasses and flowers tucked behind their ears, they roamed at will along forest trails. Ambling in the pastures near the Govardhana Hill, these two unvanquished heroes, whom even the gods worshiped, partook joyously of the unpretentious pursuits of the wandering herders whose life they now shared.

Before long they reached the Bhandira fig tree, which was the most richly branched of all fig trees. The two brothers brave as lions were joined there by the other herder boys in a boisterous series of games. They waged mock combats and tried out their slings.

Unfortunately, the wind demon Pralamba had also come there. He had disguised himself so that he looked no different from the other boys, and he was welcomed without suspicion. Wearing a herder's garments and garlanded like the rest with woodland flowers, Pralamba pleased Krishna and Balarama with his exuberance. Believing that this demon was one of their kinsmen, the herder boys let him join their contests.

During every game, Pralamba kept his cruel gaze on Krishna and Balarama as he furtively sought to spot some weak point. Finally he concluded that Krishna was too strong for him and decided to take on Balarama. The herders wanted to see how high everyone could jump, so they divided into two teams and paired off, each boy jumping at once, trying to best his rival. This way, everyone was competing against someone of comparable age and stature. Krishna competed against a boy named Sridama and Balarama against Pralamba. Krishna beat Sridama and Balarama defeated Pralamba. In fact, Krishna's side won in every case. Undaunted, the losers cheerfully boosted the victors onto their shoulders to carry them back to the Bhandira fig tree. But Pralamba tossed Balarama up onto his shoulders and went running off in the opposite direction. Straining under Balarama's weight, Pralamba started growing in size until he seemed as large as the Bhandira fig tree. At last his huge demonic form was fully revealed. Gleaming darkly like a mountain of black soot, adorned with garlands and ornaments and wearing a bright five-pointed crown that lit up his face, he shone like a stormcloud crested by the sun. Huge-headed, huge-necked, frightful as Death, wild with rage, his eyes large as wagon wheels, he made the earth shudder under his tread. Pralamba advanced like a tidal wave intent on drowning all the world. He had swept Balarama away like a black cloud carrying off the moon and had even clouded Balarama's mind.

"Krishna!" Balarama called out. "I am being carried off by a demon who made us think he was a herder boy. How can I subdue him now that he has grown so large?"

Krishna smiled, for he knew Balarama's true strength. "You are relying only on your human powers," Krishna shouted back. "Remember that deep secret, that you are actually the soul of all worlds at their dissolution! By yourself, know yourself as the soul of the primal waters at the emergence of all worlds. Recall that the activities of the ancient gods, of the creator god Brahma, and of the waters have evolved from you. Recall yourself as the first body. Your head was the sky, your body was water, your power of endurance was the earth. Fire came from

14. *Pralamba Carries Off Balarama*

your mouth, the wind was your breath, the era-creator was your mind. In truth, you have a thousand mouths, a thousand bodies, a thousand pairs of feet, a thousand pairs of eyes, a thousand flowerlike navels, a thousand shining rays. You can destroy your enemies at will. The gods in Indra's heaven can see only what you let be seen. Who can uncover more than you have previously said? All that can be known in this world you have proclaimed. You know things many gods cannot know. These lesser gods cannot see your true self. They worship only your embodied forms, which you have created out of yourself. They cannot see your bounds, so in awe they call you *Ananta*, Limitless. You are subtle, vast, one; hard to grasp even by subtle minds. Like a mountainous pillar supporting this world, you are the unmoved source of all that moves. You give form to the four oceans. You comprehend the four divisions of society and rule the four ages. You consume the food offered at rituals. Whatever I am, so you are too. For we are both eternal and of one body, though divided into two persons to help the world. Why do you still hesitate? Strike down this enemy of the gods. Strike him on the head with your thunderbolt-like fist!"

Stout-armed Balarama now sensed within himself the strength that energizes all the three worlds. With his fist tightly clenched he smashed in the top of Pralamba's head, and the demon fell to his knees. Pralamba's lifeless body lay spread out on the ground, ripped open as easily as a cloud in the sky. From his head blood flowed like a stream red with ores emerging from a mountain gorge.

Balarama came and hugged Krishna. Then Krishna and the other herders and the gods in the heavens rejoiced, praising Balarama's great strength. The gods declared, "This demon was destroyed by a boy of astonishing strength. He should be called *Baladeva*, Lord of Strength." So people came to know Balarama also by the name Baladeva, bestowed on him because he had slain the god-defying Pralamba.

❧ IV ❧

How the Govardhana Hill Was Lifted Up

KRISHNA and Balarama had many adventures during the rainy season as they roamed the woods and fields. One day when they returned home they discovered the herders excitedly preparing for the annual Indra festival. His curiosity suddenly aroused, Krishna asked, "What is this Indra festival that delights you so?"

An old herder answered. "My boy," he said, "Indra is Lord of the Thirty Gods and master of the clouds. Indra can bring rain, and if he is pleased by our sacrifices, he delights the whole world in return. When the earth is refreshed by rain, the world is as sweet-smelling as nectar. Our cows and bulls are strengthened by the new grass, and soon the cows give birth to calves and produce milk. Wherever cows have sufficient grass and fodder, people are not tormented by hunger.

"Indra milks the heavenly milk-rich cows of the sun, and they pour forth their fresh milk into waves of clouds. When fully laden the clouds make a great sound, like that of Indra's thunderbolt. This sound is carried by the wind, which quickly brings the clouds this way. Then, with blows from his thunderbolt, Indra the mountain-splitter rips open the clouds to unloose their floods.

"Indra moves about in the sky attended by clouds like a king attended by servants. Sometimes these clouds form a solid, gray mass. Sometimes they are scattered about. From these clouds when they are filled by the cows of the sun, Indra milks rain for the benefit of all. So during the rainy season all the rulers of the earth joyfully worship the ruler of the gods with sacrifices, and we do too."

Krishna had listened attentively to the old cowherd. But even though he knew the importance of Indra, Krishna replied, "Old man, we are cowherds. We make our living wandering the wooded hills with our cattle. For us, cows and hills and wild meadows are themselves godlike. Farmers live by their crops. Shop-keepers support themselves buying and selling. But for us, the cow is the principal means of livelihood. The ancient scriptures say that the particular skill a person possesses should be for that person the highest divinity. Whoever does an action proper for another and enjoys the benefit of it will reap two misfortunes: one in this life, the other in the next.

"The cleared fields that farmers till are bordered by the wooded pasturelands where we herders graze our cattle. Hilly regions are no good for crops. So for us they are a constant refuge. Some people say our hills can even change their shapes at will. Delighting in their own slopes in the forms of shaggy-maned lions or sharp-clawed tigers, the hills protect their forests by scaring away people who might come to cut down trees. If people do injure the woods, the hills disguised as wild beasts may eat those people.

"Brahmans are devoted to their scriptures and rites. Farmers worship their furrows. And herders like us who rely on the woods and hills should perform a rite for them. Let's find a good spot in the woods or at the base of a tree or on a hill. We can slaughter some clean animals suitable for sacrifice. All our cows must be milked. Then we should deck our herds with autumn flowers, parade around Govardhana, and go back to the woods to graze.

"In this autumn season everything is pleasurable. The rains have brought plenty of sweet grass to help our cows thrive. The lush woodlands are bright with charming flowers in some places, in others dark with stands of reeds. Peacocks have now grown silent. All the trees thick with foliage, which had been shaken by the monsoon gales, are calm. The sky looks like a new-crowned king, his white turban made of rain-spent clouds, with wild geese beating their wings to serve as his fly-whisk bearers, the full moon seeming like his spotless royal parasol. As the clouds scatter, streams become shallower and seem to laugh with the cries of wild geese and cranes flocking to them. Rivers speed to the ocean like a wife to her husband. White, night-blooming lilies in the lakes resemble stars in the night sky; indeed, the stars and lilies seem to be smiling at one another. At this season, one's heart delights in the fields ringing with the cries of excited curlews and pale with ripened rice. The reservoirs, pools, and flooded fields, the lakes, ponds, and streams glow with full-blown lotuses. They rear up from the mud to lift their blossoms free above the glimmering water, some coppery red, some white, some deep blue. The lake is full. The winds have died. The sky is clear. Even aroused young peacocks now are content. Instead the earth seems to have many eyes, being strewn with feathers lost by peacocks in their bristling courting dance.

"The Yamuna at this season flows restrained, her muddy flanks laced with flowery vines and dotted with geese and cranes. As seeds and fruit ripen in the meadows and woods, the birds sing madly, having so much to eat. The grain that was set growing when the rains came has grown ripe and hard. The bright autumn moon, rid of its cloud covering, ranges happily through a clear sky. Cows are twice as rich in milk, bulls are twice as lusty, trees are doubly weighted down with fruit. The land abounds in good things, the night sky is studded with stars, the waters are filled with lotuses, and people's hearts have become tranquil. In a clear sky the sun rises brilliant, its crisp rays banishing dampness. And on earth proud rulers, knowing that dry roads allow the movement of armies, are glaring angrily at each other and making ready for battle.

"The forest with its red Bandhujiva flowers is a delight. It is glorious too with yellow Asana and purple Kovidara blossoms. Autumn is strolling about the countryside like a beautiful woman. The gods are awakening from slumber, signaling the end of Indra's wild time of tumult. The rains have ended and much good grain has been secured. We should celebrate this season by honoring the godlike Govardhana Hill and especially our cows. Let's decorate our cows' horns, set peacock feathers on their heads, hang bells about their necks, and drape them with garlands of wild flowers. Let our cows be worshiped and a rite for our hill be performed. Let Indra's thirty attendant gods praise him; we should honor our hill. Actually, I could force you to do it. But all I will say is this. If you are fond of me, as we are comrades, hear me. Cows deserve every honor from all people at all times. Praising cows with ritual hymns will add to your own exaltation. Why debate? Let's begin!"

As they listened to Krishna, the herders, whose cows were their whole livelihood, were thrilled. Drinking in his words like nectar, they responded without hesitation. "We know you are a wise young man," they said. "We have learned to depend on you as our refuge, our delight and counselor. You alone have been our champion in times of anguish. Because of your deeds, Krishna, this camp has been saved from terror, and peace has come to dwell here. Ever since your birth, your manner and actions have amazed us all. In strength and valor, you are certainly first among mortals, just as Indra is among the Thirty Gods. With your generous, smiling face, you are as unrivaled on earth as the moon is in the sky.

Your charm and accomplishments as a child may have been equaled by Shiva's son Kartikeya, but certainly not by any other human child.

"Only if the ocean could leap from its bed could we resist your urging. We shall do what you suggest. Indra will still be honored by all, but we shall particularly reverence our hill because it benefits us and our cows. Let dishes of delectable sweets be prepared. There should be gleaming jugs of milk and bowls of rice mixed with milk and platters of meat. For this, we must slaughter some water buffaloes and other animals. Surely we can be ready in three days if everyone helps."

Soon the whole settlement rang with joyous sounds. The tuning of musical instruments, the bellowing of bulls, and the lowing of calves all quickened the herders' excitement. Lakes of yoghurt, whirlpools of clarified butter, rivers of sweet milk were set in motion. Great quantities of meat and mountains of gleaming rice were made ready. All the herders, accompanied by their cattle, began preparing to honor the Govardhana Hill. Everyone felt elated.

When all was ready the herders, assisted by brahman priests, performed the ritual for the hill. The grain, milk, fine yoghurt, and meat that were offered to the hill were consumed by Krishna, who had by his magical power become the hill. The principal brahmans were served next, and they ate until they were completely satisfied, after which they pronounced a benediction. Krishna in his human form then ate and drank milk to his heart's content and finally said with a smile, "I am satisfied."

Seeing Krishna seated atop the hill, seeing him there wreathed in garlands, daubed with pastes, looking himself like the hill, the chief herders approached him reverently. Magically, Krishna could also be seen bowing together with these herders at the foot of the hill. In wonder, the herders said to him as he sat godlike atop this splendid hill, "Lord, we are your slaves. What can we do to please you?"

Speaking for the hill, Krishna said to them, "From now on I, your hill, should be worshiped if you wish well toward your cattle. I should be for you the principal god, for I can satisfy your every desire. Because of me, your hill, you will henceforth possess tens of thousands of cows. I will be gracious to all herders who worship me. Being pleased with Nanda and other far-famed herders, I shall grant you vast wealth. Let all the cows and calves approach me. This will be for me the utmost bliss."

So the herders with their cows and bulls walked around that excellent hill to

15. *Krishna Hunts Animals Suitable for Sacrifice*

16. The Herders Reverence the Govardhana Hill

purify themselves. Cows by hundreds and by thousands along with their calves ran forward happily. They were profusely garlanded, and their horns were twined with flowers. The herders followed, driving the cattle forward. With their bodies streaked with colored pastes and clad in red, yellow, and dark garments, with peacock-colored armbands and peacock feathers fixed in their hairbands, the cowherds thronged forward. Some rode on bulls. Others danced ecstatically. Others guided the fast-moving cows.

When this homage of the cows was completed, the Krishna seated atop the hill disappeared. Then together with Krishna the herders returned to their camp. Krishna was delighted to have inaugurated this splendid celebration of the Govardhana Hill.

Indra, however, was enraged that his festival had been halted, and he spoke his mind to a troop of his stormclouds. "Listen to me, my fine sky elephants!" he roared. "Nanda and the other herders in Vrindavana are so devoted to Krishna that they have become hostile to my festival. I know they live by their cows, so let's torment those cows with wind and rain for seven days and nights. I myself, mounted on my great elephant Airavata, shall unloose these storms with my thunderbolt. When all their cows and calves have been destroyed by frightful rains and fierce gales, then the herders themselves shall die of want!"

Soon, amidst dreadful roaring, destruction-bearing stormclouds as big as mountains began covering over the sky. The heavy clouds rampaged about like a herd of elephants. They slithered across the sky like crocodiles or snakes. They made the day like night. They flung down torrents not in separate drops but in streams, as though spouted from an elephant's trunk or poured from a bamboo pipe. To those below it seemed as though the very ocean, boundless and fathomless, had risen into the heavens. Birds hid, and animals fled, as the mountain-like clouds roared all about in the sky. The cruel clouds blotted out the sun, moon, and stars above, while below, waters mangled the earth. Peacocks screeched, smaller birds chattered feebly. Swelling over their banks, rivers carried off large trees. Grasses and trees trembled as if from fright as the clouds howled and the rains thundered. "The end of the world has come! The earth is sinking beneath the sea!" the terrified herders cried. Cows stood unmoving, their faint lowing almost like weeping. Their ears and thighs were stiff, their heads and hooves motionless, the hair on their wet bodies bristling, their bellies and udders withered by hunger. Some cows and calves died, overcome by exhaustion, dampness, or illness. Other cows stood over their calves trying to shelter them. Fallen, trembling, overwhelmed by rain, many calves turned their eyes toward Krishna. "Please save us," their wan faces seemed to say.

Seeing the downcast faces of the herders and the havoc brought on the herds by this vast storm, Krishna became incensed. Then he thought exultantly, "I shall lift up Govardhana! With its wide-spreading groves and pastures, it will make a splendid refuge from the rain. If I hold up Govardhana, the hill, under my control, will form an earthen roof and save the cows and herders."

Krishna, whose strength was vast; Krishna, himself like a mountain; Krishna, Vishnu on earth, then calmly lifted up the hill with his left hand. Loose rocks were sent crashing down, and trees were uprooted by the jolt. Its crags were revolving and falling all about, but the hill nonetheless ascended to the skies. "Does that hill have wings?" wondered the gods overhead.

Raised up with the clouds that surrounded it, the hill became the roof of a spacious shelter. Indra's tumultuous torrents continued to rake Govardhana's slopes, filling its streams, tossing stones, and making the whole hill tremble. But down below, the people of Vrindavana could not see or hear the cloudbursts or the rock showers or the wind's howling. Their force broken by the hill, the rains became gentle streams on the lower slopes, bringing beauty and luxuriance so that the hill looked as resplendent as a peacock. The hill's streams were flecked with gold and black ores. Shaken trees had strewn the hill with flowers of every color. Cobras, which had been disturbed, slithered down, their great hoods flared, flicking their double tongues. Zigzag markings gleamed on their sides. Birds filled the sky, flying up and down ceaselessly in their confusion. Angry lions roared like water-laden stormclouds, and the hollow growls of tigers echoed like a thudding churn.

Some outcroppings were covered by clouds, others half covered, others intertwined with the clouds. Every contour had been altered. Easy slopes had been made impassable, and others made more accessible. But all in all, this different Govardhana was more charming than ever.

Assaulted by all that rain, the hill looked dazed, like the city of Tripura when Shiva besieged it. With its cave mouths closed by clouds, the hill seemed asleep in the sky, pillowed in Krishna's uplifted palm. No birds called now in the trees, no peacocks cried in the groves. Raised on Krishna's rodlike arm, the hill was like an umbrella held up against the massed blue-black clouds. The hill's trembling rim and quaking heights made the trees and woods shiver as if from fever. The cloud-ravaged hill in Krishna's palm was like a country scarred by a monarch's fast-spinning chariot wheels. The clouds crowned the hill like a high city towering above a plain.

With the hill settled firmly in his palm, Krishna spoke to the herders. "With powers beyond the Thirty Gods' imagining," he explained, smiling, "I have made Govardhana a refuge from Indra's gales. Bring your cows in quickly. Let space be apportioned by mutual agreement, according to region and convenience, taking into account the size of each person's herd. There is room for all. The shelter I have made by lifting up this hill could hold all the three worlds, so it will surely hold Vrindavana."

17. *Krishna Lifts the Govardhana Hill*

The herders burst into joyous shouts that merged with the cows' lowing and the sounds of thunder far overhead. Then the cows, divided into separate herds, came in under that hill, which Krishna was guiding tenderly with one hand as if it were a favorite guest. Bringing along their storm-endangered belongings and their yoked carts, the herders entered the shelter formed by the hill.

Indra now could see that Krishna was doing something beyond the power of all the lesser gods, beyond even his own great power, and he relinquished his resolution and called off his stormclouds. Ending the seven-day ordeal, the Lightning Hurler and his cloud attendants all departed for the heavens. The sun, which Indra had hidden for seven dark days, glowed once again in a cloudless sky. No longer dispirited, the cows left the refuge by the same path they had come and returned to their stables in the village. Krishna, fulfiller of wishes, himself strong as any mountain, then placed the hill back securely on its foundations.

When he saw Krishna holding up Govardhana, Indra was awed and wanted to pay his respects. So he came down to earth astride the great elephant Airavata. His temples still dampened by a few last drops of *mada* fluid, Airavata was as pale-colored as a spent rain cloud. Resplendent in his divine garlands and pastes, Indra wore on his head a crown that crackled with lightning.

He found Krishna seated on a rock near the Govardhana Hill and recognized at once that this boy, though dressed like a herder, was in fact Vishnu. For on Krishna's chest, which was as dark as a forest of palmyra palms, Indra could see Vishnu's divine curl of hair. And overhead, invisible to human eyes, Garuda, king of birds, was shading Krishna from the hot sun with his extended wings. Dismounting from Airavata, mighty Indra approached Krishna respectfully.

"Krishna," he said, "when I sent my devastating gales, you, out of love for cows, did something beyond the power of all other gods. I myself was pleased by your deed. Who would not have been impressed to see you lift that hill, like a house in the sky? I was furious when my festival was disrupted, so I afflicted these cows with a seven-day deluge. No one but Vishnu could have withstood me, and I see clearly now that you are indeed Vishnu, come to earth on some mission for the gods. Acting as a mortal human being but with Vishnu's incomparable strength, you must accomplish all you undertake. Who but Vishnu among all the gods and worlds could bear such a weight? As the strongest of a team of oxen is placed in the lead when a heavy yoke is sunk down, so are you depended on by other gods when they encounter difficulties. As gold is prized over all other metals so are you, great Vishnu, held best in all the universe. In wisdom and even in age, Brahma cannot keep pace with you any more than a cripple can run. As the Himalayas are the greatest mountains, as the ocean is the greatest body of water, as Garuda is the foremost of winged creatures, so are you best of the immortals.

"From you I have learned many things: that waters float below the earth, and that above the waters stand elephants who hold up the earth's surface where human beings live. Above is the sky where birds fly. Above the sky is the sun, the gleaming door of heaven. Beyond the sun lies the celestial world where I preside. Beyond my world, Brahma sits among his hosts of seers. Here the moon and planets roam. But beyond even Brahma's world is Goloka, a world graced by cows. Goloka is of all the heavens the highest, for it is made resplendent by your own presence. Even from Brahma we could learn nothing of this cow world.

"The dreadful lower world is for evildoers. The earth is the field of moral action where good or bad deeds are done. The sky is the realm of the wind and of other such unsteady things. My world is attained after death by persons of self-discipline who do good deeds while on earth. Brahma's higher world is for those who truly radiate the energy acquired through self-denial. But even these may not reach the highest realm, Goloka, which you have established as your own. I am renowned as Lord of the Thirty Gods, and am called the City-Destroyer, but I cannot match your radiance. Nonetheless, once we two were both born sons of Aditi, and at that time I was your elder brother. Remembering this, please forgive the harshness shown you by my clouds.

"Now hear what Brahma, the creator, and the cows in the sky have to say. The cows of heaven are protected by you, and the worlds are protected by these cows. 'We cows,' they wish to say, 'are overjoyed by your protection. Now we, increasing together with bulls and our offspring, will supply people with oxen to draw their carts. We shall help people gratify the gods with the gift of butter for sacred fires. Our dung, moreover, will enrich and purify. Great Krishna, you are our guide, our very life. From now on you will be our lord!'

"So," Indra said, once again speaking for himself, "I shall now sprinkle you with water from these brimming golden jugs. I shall remain Lord of the Thirty Gods, but you will be Lord of Cows. You will be praised by the name *Govinda,*

Lord of Cows. The gods I command will still call me *Mahendra,* Great Indra, but you they shall now call *Upendra,* a second Indra, for you have been placed above me, as a lord, by the cows.

"Listen further. My rainy season lasts four months. I now relinquish its latter half to you. From today, people will think of the first two months only as mine. In the heavy early rains, my standard will still be worshiped. Then when your season comes, the sun will once again send forth its glowing rays. Peacocks made haughty by my thunder will grow calm, their wild shrieks dwindling. Though peacocks are silent, water-loving birds will dive and glide about, and herons will call excitedly. Bulls will be made wild with lust, and the cows they satisfy will give milk abundantly. In the bright sky, geese will soar like arrows. Below, lotuses will crowd the lakes and ponds. Rice will ripen in the fields. The retreats of holy men will be well provisioned. Every country in the world will be agreeable, with flooded streams returning to their channels, muddy roads made passable, groves heavy with fruit, and fields lush with ripening sugar cane. The world will fill with festivals."

Indra then took pots brimming with celestial water and consecrated Krishna as Govinda, Lord of Cows. Seeing Krishna thus anointed, the cows standing beside their bulls in the sky sprinkled him with milk from their udders. Clouds released nectarlike showers to contribute to Krishna's consecration. From the trees, milky showers like moon rays seemed to fall. Flowers rained down from the sky, and musical instruments sounded. Holy men chanted. The waters drew back, and the earth once again displayed its familiar form. Winds subsided into gentleness. The sun and moon could be seen moving calmly in their customary paths. Trees sent forth new shoots. Elephants released streams of *mada* fluid from their temples, and in the woods wild beasts were elated. Mountains glistened with ores and new growth. At Krishna's consecration as Govinda, all the earth had become like Indra's paradise, where every sense is gratified.

When Indra departed for his sky realm, Krishna returned to the camp, where he was received enthusiastically. The elder herders congratulated him. "You have saved our cows from a great peril that threatened us all," they said. "Your powers are beyond those of any mortal. Your actions ever since your birth have seemed

18. Indra Pays Homage to Krishna

godlike, and this has long made us wonder. But when you lifted up that hill, we knew that you are a god. Are you one of the Thirty Gods, a Rudra or a Maruta or a Vasu? If so, why have you come among us? Why do you spend your days guiding cows through the meadows when you seem as powerful as a Lokapala, a Deva, a Danava, Yaksha, or Gandharva? Whoever you are, we feel honored to have you among us. Whatever your purpose in living here, we are now your followers.''

Hearing the elders speak in this way, lotus-eyed Krishna smilingly replied, ''You have grown accustomed to thinking of me as a kinsman, but it is true that

I am not of your blood. If you are intent on hearing of me and seeing me fully, trust to time. For now, regard me simply as a powerful friend. Why bother about knowing my immortal name while I am here among you? Please do not press me further." Respectfully, the herders fell silent and soon dispersed in various directions.

With a young, new moon sailing untroubled through the balmy autumn nights, Krishna felt playful and exuberant. Some days he pitted one lusty bull against another on the dung-daubed roads. Sometimes he urged the strongest herders to wrestle against each other. Sometimes he chased after cows in the fields, tussling them to the ground. And sometimes, stirred on by pleasurable emotions, he sported with girls from the camp through the dark, warm nights. The girls ecstatically drank in his countenance as if it were the moon come to earth. His yellow silk garments made his dark body even more alluring. With his bright armbands and wild-flower garlands, Krishna's glowing presence made all Vraja glow. Entranced by his graceful ways, the girl herders greeted him joyously as he strolled about. They pressed their full, swelling breasts against him, their eyes darting about. Eluding the restraints of mothers, fathers, and brothers, the pleasure-drunk girls dashed through the night to his side. Forming a row, they sang praises of his deeds, each girl striving to outdo the others.

Their eyes fixed on Krishna, the devoted herder girls would sometimes follow him through the fields, rhythmically clapping their hands. His dancing, his singing, his amorous, smiling glances thrilled them, and they willingly responded. Intent on their beloved, following where he led, they sang sweet songs born of their joy. Their limbs were soon covered with dust and dung as they struggled to satisfy Krishna, like excited female elephants topped by an aroused bull elephant. With wide eyes beaming with love, the deer-eyed girls thirstily drank in their lover's dark form. Then others had their chance to find pleasure in his arms. When he sighed with pleasure, the girls joyously echoed his melodious sounds. Their hair, once carefully bound and parted, lay strewn about as they fell back fulfilled, stray hairs caressing the nipples of their breasts.

On many a moonlit autumn night, Krishna and the herder girls joined in these revels, amusing themselves in delicious play. But on one such evening,

19. *Krishna Distracts a Herder Girl*

20. *Krishna's Glowing Countenance Reigns Over the Quiet Nighttime*

while Krishna was fully absorbed in the pursuit of pleasure, the bull demon Arishta came to the camp.

Grim as a cinder-black cloud, sharp-horned, red-eyed, Arishta was always prancing about on razor-edged hooves like black Death. His tongue and lips rubbed together unceasingly, his tail lashed restlessly about. The sinews of his shoulders bulged hard. His menacing hump was huge. Stale urine and excrement encrusted his limbs. He terrified cows with his coarse, fleshy mouth, his bruised face, his flailing horns, his great thighs, heavy legs, and sagging belly. Shaking with lust, horns down ready for battle, folds of skin dangling at his throat, this demon bull roamed through all of Vraja seeking out fertile young cows, forcing some to abort their newly conceived calves and frantically mounting others who had just been delivered of calves. He injured every cow he approached, for the cruel Arishta could only satisfy his lust by force.

70

Just at this time, led on by Death, Arishta was approaching the cowsheds of Vrindavana. Big-bodied, he danced forward roaring like a thundercloud, and would soon have left desolation everywhere, young bulls slain, calves dead. But Krishna came running up and distracted him by clapping his hands and roaring out a battle cry. Turning toward Krishna, Arishta excitedly lashed his tail about, bellowing out his eagerness for battle. Motionless as a mountain, Krishna stood poised like one bull opposing another as Arishta charged, head down, his horns pointed at Krishna's chest. When Arishta struck, Krishna seized hold of him. From the impact, foam exploded from Arishta's mouth and nostrils. Their limbs became so entangled that they seemed like two writhing clouds. Finally subduing the bull's overweening pride, Krishna placed his foot between the bull's horns and squeezed Arishta's neck as if it were a damp cloth. Then, uprooting his left horn, which looked like Death's own cudgel, Krishna dealt him one final blow with it full in the face. With one horn pulled out and his head and shoulders shattered, Arishta's lifeblood rushed from him like rain from a cloud.

When they saw that Krishna had killed the vicious demon bull, the people of Vrindavana were so excited they shouted for joy. With Arishta dead, lotus-eyed Krishna's glowing countenance once more reigned over the quiet nighttime. Delighted, all the herders honored Krishna as the immortals in heaven honor Indra.

❊❲ V ❳❊

King Kamsa's Snare

A S news of Krishna's deeds in Vraja spread about like wildfire, in the royal city of Mathura King Kamsa grew more and more afraid. The pulling over of two big trees by a child was an unheard-of feat and had made Kamsa fear the emergence of a deadly antagonist. Then there had been the slaying of Putana, the conquest of Kaliya, the clever destruction of Dhenuka, the downfall of Pralamba, the raising of Govardhana to give the cows refuge, challenging Indra's sway, and finally the killing of the high-humped Arishta, which had so delighted the herders. Kamsa greatly feared that his own destruction might be next. When he had heard details of the way Arishta died, Kamsa had fallen down in a dead faint.

In alarm, Kamsa called his kinsmen and advisers to a secret nighttime conference. Noble Vasudeva, Krishna's father, was summoned, and Kahva, and Kahva's truthful younger brother Daruka. Vaitarana came, and the powerful Vikadru; the distinguished Bhayesakha and the fortunate Viprithu. Also present were the generous Kritavarman and the forceful Bhurishravas. To his assembled kinsmen, Kamsa spoke these words:

"Gentlemen, you are all men of affairs, acquainted with scripture, familiar with law and custom, and active in your pursuit of the three proper ends of life, pleasure, prosperity, and righteousness. You know as well as any sage on earth what right conduct is, and you have always been eager to do the bidding of your elders. You are masters of statecraft and warfare. You are renowned for wise counsel and understanding of the distinct stages of life and classes of society. You prescribe worthy norms of conduct to others, and you yourselves prominently exemplify those norms. You are a terror to hostile nations and a comfort to those seeking aid. Persons so admirable in conduct and correct in conversation would be a credit to Indra's court; how much more so to an earthly court like mine! In demeanor you are like holy men. When angered you resemble the storm gods. In lustre you are like planets. Our great clan is held together by you heroes of far-flung fame as the surface of the earth is held together by mountains.

"Being then as you are so solicitous of my welfare, how have you failed to see a growing menace to my interests? A certain so-called Krishna, son of the Vraja cowherd Nanda, has been advancing toward my throne as fast as a thunderhead, yet none of you has warned me of him. One would think I had no ministers at all! A king with no spies is blind. This boy in Nanda's household has become dangerous, like an unnoticed ailment or an unexpected cloudburst in the dry season. All this time I knew nothing of the power or accomplishments or the real nature of this astonishing son of Nanda. Whether or not he is a god I don't know. But what he has done seems beyond the power of ordinary mortals and even of most gods. While still an infant suckling at the breast of the vulture wet nurse Putana, he sucked out her life. When the serpent Kaliya was about to drag him down beneath the Yamuna, this boy subdued him in a moment. Then Dhenuka was made to fall to his death from the top of a palmyra palm. Pralamba, whom even the gods could not face, was slain like some ordinary mortal by one blow of a boy's fist. After halting Indra's festival, Krishna foiled Indra's revenge by making a shelter for the rain-ravaged cows with the Govardhana Hill. Then he killed the fierce Arishta by pulling out one of his horns.

"This is no human youth but some god disporting himself as a boy. Tales of his deeds have made my hair stand on end. He must have killed me in a former life, for now he seems to stand before me, eager to fight me. What a contrast there is between his mean cowherd's existence and the feats he playfully performs in Vraja! Who is this god who delights in a mean life as fire does in a cremation ground? They say Vishnu at the gods' request once disguised himself as a dwarf to save the earth. While disguised as a lion, Vishnu killed Hiranyakashipu. Shiva too disguised himself when he slew the demons on the Sweta mountain. In a boar's form Vishnu lifted the earth up out of the sea. And once when the gods and demons joined forces to churn the ocean for *amarta*, the drink that gives immortality, Vishnu as a tortoise below the ocean supported the churning-stick mountain. Then, after the *amarta* was churned up, Vishnu in the form of a woman entered the battle between the gods and demons to rescue that life-bestowing drink. Another time, Vishnu was born as Rama to slay Ravana. Vishnu often assumes this or that surprising shape when it suits the purposes of the gods. This

73

21. *Gods and Demons Churn the Ocean*

boy called Krishna is probably Vishnu, or possibly Indra. Whoever he is, he may have come here to destroy me, just as Narada warned.

"I strongly suspect, moreover, that my own kinsman Vasudeva is involved in this plot against me. I recently met with Narada a second time in the Khatvanga forest. He said to me, 'Kamsa, all your efforts to destroy Devaki's eighth child were foiled by Vasudeva. The infant girl you smashed against a rock was actually the daughter of Yasoda. Devaki had given birth that night to Krishna; Krishna is Vasudeva's son. To insure your death, Vasudeva switched the two infants under cover of night. Vasudeva is your enemy though he claims to be a friend. That daughter of Yasoda is now installed among the Vindhya hills. A wish-fulfilling goddess and a slayer of demons, she is served by frightful creatures. Full-breasted, wearing armbands fashioned from brilliant peacock tails, she glows in the sky above the deep Vindhya forests. Below her, proud wild cocks and crows cry out. Herds of goats and flocks of birds abound. Lions, tigers, and wild boars in the dense woods roar challenges to one another, while above, the sounds of her attendants' musical instruments augment these roars and cries. She dwells in these jungles, rejoicing constantly, honored by the gods, a terror to her foes.'

"I thus have it on Narada's authority," Kamsa continued, "that Krishna, said to be Nanda's son, is in fact a son of Vasudeva. Vasudeva's two sons, Narada says, wish to murder me and my brother. These sons of Vasudeva are cousins of mine and by rights should be allies. But in their hearts they hate me. Like a crow that alights on your head and pecks out your eyes with its flesh-greedy beak—that is what I now discover Vasudeva and his sons are. I have always cherished Vasudeva as befits an elder of my own family, and outwardly he treated me as a son. Yet, though always dealt with tenderly by me, he plots my downfall. One can even make amends for causing an abortion or the death of a cow or a woman. But someone who shows ingratitude, especially to a relative, will surely end up in hell.

"Let me say this to any of you who might think of speaking in defense of this villain: Remember, when wild elephants fight in the jungle, the underbrush gets trampled. And when they finish fighting, the elephants together consume what they have smashed. I warn you, when a family feud breaks out, those who try to mediate are crushed.

"Vasudeva, you are a compulsive conniver. I was stupid to let you have a place of honor. White hairs alone cannot make a person venerable. Only one whose understanding is mature deserves that name. You are old in years but mean-minded and ill-informed, as useless as a spent rain cloud. Didn't you think to yourself, 'With Kamsa out of the way, my son will rule in Mathura'? But you have schemed in vain, you foolish old man. No one who opposes me can hope to live!

"Vasudeva, you have always been in our household, honored by my father, indeed by all, as the senior member of our clan. Obviously, through the treachery of such a leading personage, our whole clan has been made blameworthy. By plotting my end and setting up Krishna as my rival, you have forfeited any claim on our loyalty. Yet I have never killed a priest, an old man, or a woman, certainly never one who was a relative. Nor will I do so now. Because of your age you will be spared. But your sons must die. Our clan will never know peace as long as Krishna and I are both alive.

"My plan is to ask Akrura to fetch Nanda and the other herders here from Vraja. Tell them, Akrura, they are all ordered to come to Mathura at once to pay their annual harvest tribute. You should further explain to everyone in Vraja that when they come, they will witness a great athletic festival dedicated to our famed archer's bow. Urge all the herders, therefore, to bring their cows with them to Mathura and stable them nearby so that our invited guests can enjoy fresh milk and butter. Akrura, you should then state that the king and his attendants and priests particularly desire to see Krishna and Balarama, as they have heard that these two are expert wrestlers, hard-limbed and skillful. Say that the king's two best court wrestlers stand ready to challenge them, and that I naturally wish to see these two godlike youths because they are my cousins even though they have been living all this time as cowherds in Vraja. Go quickly, Akrura. I am determined to lay eyes on these two. If you can get them to come here, I can do the rest. If they won't come willingly, I shall have them seized. But first we should try enticing them. Trusty Akrura, I beg you to undertake this difficult assignment as a favor to me —that is, if you are not yourself in league with Vasudeva!''

Krishna's father had stood as unshaken as the sea during Kamsa's self-serving tirade. The only emotion it had stirred in him was compassion, and he made no attempt to defend himself. Most of the others present, seeing him thus vilified, only averted their eyes or muttered a few inaudible words of disapproval. But Akrura sensed how the gods were shaping events without Kamsa's knowledge, and he readily acceded to Kamsa's request. Thrilled by the prospect of soon seeing lotus-eyed Krishna, he departed at once like a thirsty man who has sighted water.

Of those who remained in the assembly hall, most simply covered their ears with their hands, assuming Vasudeva's fate was sealed. But fearless old Andhaka spoke up. Without displaying any external sign of anger, Andhaka said to Kamsa, "My son, the wise condemn this kind of conduct, especially toward a relative. Remember the saying, 'One who is not truly a Yadava cannot be made one by force.' You have turned from the traditions of our Yadava ancestors and disgraced your line. It does not matter that you are Ugrasena's son. Whatever your family name, you are what you are. A head is the same whether shaven or covered with matted locks. Ugrasena is to be pitied for having such a son as you.

"The wise never proclaim their own virtues. If one's virtues are genuine,

22. *Kamsa Instructs Akrura to Bring Krishna and Balarama to Mathura*

others will praise them. Your immature, clan-destroying conduct has brought
the Yadavas into disrepute everywhere. By words alone no goal is attained, nor is
anyone's true character revealed. Do you think slandering a virtuous old man is
more excusable than killing a brahman? The elderly should be approached as
cautiously as fire, because like fire their anger can enter and devastate internal
worlds. A bungled ritual can harm the sacrificer; so it is with abuse of the old.
Forethought would have curbed your rashness. A self-disciplined person can learn
about human perversity without sharing it, as one watches from above the move-
ments of a fish in water.

"You should not blame Vasudeva for his son's fearsome deeds. The cruelty
of a son does not imply the cruelty of his father. Such cruelty may cause his father

nothing but sorrow. Vasudeva, it is true, did hide his infant son. But if you think that was improper, is not Ugrasena even more at fault for not destroying you in infancy? Sons save their fathers from unhappiness after death. This is why the wise all tell us, 'Beget sons!'

"Every one of us trembles to see Vasudeva slandered and Krishna angered. Moreover, many inauspicious omens have already foreboded danger to you. There are vicious snakes about. People have had strange dreams, coming just at night's end, which seem to hint that our city will soon be widowed by the death of her king. The planet Mars has come close to the star Arcturus. Birds cry out shrilly. The she-jackal who normally scavenges around cremation grounds now comes eagerly morning and evening right up to the city gates, howling constantly. A meteor has crashed onto the surface of the earth. Mountain summits have been shaken by an earthquake. Foul mists obscure the rising sun. Birds and animals are acting oddly and making strange sounds. With the sun covered over, only a lurid bloodred flickering lightning pierces the gloom. Thunder has shaken gods from their seats and birds from the trees but no rain has followed. Dry lightning and thunder are grim portents. In fact, all the signs that prophets say mean the imminent death of a king have been seen.

"Kamsa, you have been spiteful to your own kin. You have scorned royal duties and become angered for no reason, making others fear you. You have stupidly abused a respected elder who has always kept his word. Kamsa, we cannot reverence a person who is bad for our clan. Akrura will soon bring lotus-eyed Krishna here. Krishna will reunite this clan that you have split.

"You could still save yourself. Vasudeva would surely excuse what you have just said as the ravings of a clouded mind. If your wits are restored, go yourself with Vasudeva to Krishna's camp and humbly make your peace with him." Kamsa heard Andhaka out, his eyes slowly reddening with rage. Then without a word he stalked off, and the king's kinsmen returned home deeply troubled.

In keeping with his instructions and his own desires, Akrura was already speeding in his horse-drawn chariot swift as the mind toward Vrindavana. Krishna too experienced a premonition that a relative worthy of respect equal to that due a father would soon arrive.

But at that very hour, the long-fanged horse demon Keshin was also nearing Vrindavana. Furious, immensely vile, an eater of human flesh, Keshin roamed where he chose unchecked. Any region he entered soon resembled a cremation ground heaped up with human bones. He rent the earth with his hooves, toppling trees in his pell-mell rush. His braying rivaled the wind, his leaping awed the sky. Meadows were turned into deserts by his lightning-like assaults, and woodlands were devastated, made useless for any human being or cow. Anyone found in his path was ravenously ripped apart and eaten. This powerful aroused horse, his mane wild, was headed for Vrindavana at Kamsa's bidding to destroy Krishna and wreak havoc on the herders.

When they saw him the men and women of the settlement took their children and ran off shouting for Krishna's help. Hearing their cries, Krishna ran forward. Keshin arched his neck, braying stridently, and with eyes and teeth gleaming, he rushed right at Krishna. Krishna loomed before him like a cloud before the moon. Fearing that Keshin was about to devour Krishna, the herders called out, "Krishna, you are too young to tangle with that killer horse. He is Kamsa's ally and cannot be overcome!" But Krishna was steadfast.

Keshin was now dashing about the woodland furiously kicking down trees. His muscles pulsed like waves or rolling clouds. Rage-engendered sweat fell from his brow, long mane, and heavily built shoulders. White foam flowed from his mouth until the air seemed frosted by a winter fog. Braying, he drenched Krishna with a spray of spittle. Krishna's hair was colored red by the finely powdered plumes of dust stirred up by Keshin's sharp hind hooves. Then he darted toward Krishna, gnashing his teeth, and struck with his forelegs at Krishna's chest. Again and again he drove his heels into Krishna's side, and with his sharp teeth he bit into Krishna's arm. Tangling with Krishna, his mane flying about, he seemed like the sun half obscured by a cloud. Made furious by Krishna's nimbleness, Keshin redoubled his efforts and tried to kill Krishna by crushing him under his belly. But Krishna was stronger. He gripped that proud beast's head with his arms. Held thus in a headlock, unable to eat Krishna, Keshin instead began vomiting out blood and spittle. He could not get at Krishna with either hooves or teeth. Trying to turn his head about to see his tormentor, Keshin, the brayer of destruction, the spiller of blood, the dispenser of terror, reared up repeatedly on his hind legs, his excrement and urine flowing, his tail lashing out, his coat beaded with sweat. Trying vainly to free himself, he gradually exhausted his strength. Keshin's weary

23. *Krishna Battles the Horse Demon Keshin*

head, held fast in Krishna's arms, shone now no brighter than the moon when, at the end of the hot season, it sinks spent, half wrapped in cloud, onto Mount Meru at night's end. Shaken loose by Krishna's grip, Keshin's once flashing teeth had fallen out, scattering like the fragments of a spent autumnal cloud.

Keshin was no more. Split by Krishna's arm, Keshin's body resembled that of an animal fearfully sundered by Shiva's bow. Keshin had been split in half from head to tail. One ear, one eye, half a lip could be seen on either side. But Krishna's arm, injured though it had been by Keshin's teeth, was still magnificent. It looked like some ancient palm tree scarred by the tusks of jungle elephants. Lotus-eyed Krishna stood beside Keshin's torn carcass, calmly smiling.

Seeing that Keshin had been slain, the herder men and women all became

80

ecstatic. Everyone of every age and rank congratulated Krishna time and again in words welling from exquisite joy. "What a fine thing," they exclaimed, "to have rid Vraja of that horse! He had killed many herders and children, many cows and calves and other animals. He had gone everywhere he wished, scourging the earth as though trying to destroy the human race. No one could stand against him, not even gods, much less any mortal!" When they finished praising him, Krishna returned with them to Vrindavana.

The sun was growing large as it went to rest. Evening reddened the land. The moon's softly glowing disc was just beginning its ascent. Here and there planets emitted their calm beams. The herders had now drawn within their enclosures, as night predators set out in search of prey. The cows had returned home and were being milked by the herders. As they were milked, the cows lowed incessantly, gazing toward their calves who were tied at a distance from them. In the early dusk, red Sakragopa beetles flickered like refracted extensions of the setting sun. In the distant huts of forest hermits, chanting could be heard and glowing fires glimpsed. In the herder camp flickered numerous fires made with dried cow dung or wood carried in by the herders on their shoulders. The large moon, once risen above the horizon, glowed clearly. The night deepened as day departed. With the sun gone, the moon's brilliance intensified. On earth, sacrificial fires were lit, and fires and moonglow blended and merged. As the sun's last rays faded, myriads of stars slowly brightened, making the sky resemble a burnt-over mountain where scattered fires still smouldered.

Akrura delighted in each detail of this peaceful scene as he neared Vrindavana in his wind-swift chariot. Entering the herder settlement, he asked urgently of everyone he met the way to Nanda's home. Guided to Nanda's compound, Akrura dismounted and entered on foot. When he passed through the gate, he came first to where the cows were being milked. There Akrura saw young Krishna seeming like a bull standing amidst the young calves. In a stammering voice suffused with awed excitement Akrura exclaimed, "O dearest Krishna!" Gazing insatiably at this stableyard scene, so filled with tenderness and well-being, Akrura inwardly poured out praises for the superb youth standing there. "At last I have seen lotus-eyed, lionhearted Krishna," he thought. "Dark as a rain-filled cloud or a finely wooded hill, with Vishnu's sacred curl of hair on his chest still un-scarred by war; his two long arms finely ornamented, though he stands so humbly here; could this be Vishnu secretly incarnate in this body humbly wrapped in a herder's clothes? The wreath on his head glows like a crown. His ears are embellished with earrings. A splendid necklace rests on his broad chest. Also like Vishnu, he is wearing yellow garments and has long, shapely arms and a body capable of arousing passion in women by the thousand. Surely this is Vishnu, protector and refuge of the universe, subduer of enemies, bestrider of the three worlds. His fine hand seems suited for Vishnu's bright discus; his other hand, uplifted, calls for Vishnu's club. Surely the supreme lord has come down to this very place. This herder boy can certainly revive Mathura's fortunes. Indeed, our clan will be enhanced by his fame a hundred-, a thousandfold, like the ocean made vast by the multitudes of streams entering it. Having come to earth, he must in time subject the world to his will. He would not reign in the manner of an earthly ruler but stand far above all kings. As he once strode conquering across all Indra's heaven in three steps, so now he will stride across this land restoring old King Ugrasena's righteous rule. All enmity and greed will be wiped away, as foretold in the ancient prophesies.

"Though I shall always honor him in my heart as Vishnu," Akrura reflected, "I believe I should treat him simply as Vasudeva's son when I deliver Kamsa's message. Only his human guise may be evident to people here if they have not seen as I have been blessed to see, with eyes divinely opened."

For these prudent reasons, Akrura gave no hint that he knew Krishna's true identity as he announced his presence. When he explained that he had brought a message from the king, a number of the older herders were called to Nanda's home to hear him. But before they arrived, Akrura spoke confidentially to Krishna and Balarama.

"Vasudeva has been badly abused," Akrura confided. "Even though he is near the end of his life and has begun to feel the enfeeblement of age, Kamsa maliciously torments him. Much distressed by your long absence, Vasudeva knows no peace, day or night. Krishna, you are also sorely missed by gentle Devaki, who has no sons to press to her breast. She has grown thin grieving for her lost children. Like a cow who has lost her calf she longs for another glimpse of you. Her eyes weary from weeping, she dresses in dingy clothes, shunning finery. The inner glow that once lit up her face like the moon has been eclipsed.

82

She wishes always, always for your return. And it is for the lost sounds of your infant chatter that she sighs, because she does not know how handsome you have become, your face bright as the moon. In her present state, what solace is her child to Devaki? Perhaps it would be better if she had never given birth to a son. A mother who has no child knows only a single sorrow. But a woman who has no joy from her son is ever newly grieved. Surely a woman with such a son as you, excellent as Indra, ought not to have to grieve.

"Krishna, if you cherish the mother who once carried you as the earth does now, you should lift her up out of this ocean of misery. Nor should you forget much-reviled old Vasudeva. As you subdued the dreadful Kaliya in the waters of the Yamuna and lifted the expansive Govardhana Hill and destroyed the haughty Arishta and killed the evil Keshin; with a similar effort you should rescue these two from their distress. All who saw your father reviled by Kamsa shed many tears. So many babies have been torn from Devaki, yet despite her feelings she must obey Kamsa. Kamsa has deprived your parents of all their children. Debts to one's parents should be repaid, Krishna. You should show mercy to your father and mother in their time of sorrow. Saving them would be a matchless act."

When Akrura had finished, Krishna, with no sign of anger, said only, "So be it."

Akrura next told the assembled elders that they must come to Mathura to pay their customary yearly taxes and that they should also bring their herds along with them to provide milk and butter for the king's athletic festival. Taking account of the size of each person's herd, they then worked out a way to pay Kamsa's tax with the milk and butter of their cows and buffaloes. When the tax and their other offerings had been agreed upon, they returned home to make ready for the trek to the city in obedience to the orders of the king.

After the elders had left, Akrura passed the night with Krishna and Balarama, recounting to them all that had happened in Mathura.

❈{ VI }❈

On to Mathura

THE pure air at daybreak thronged with the sounds of birds. A web of moon rays faded in the west as the sky became suffused with the dawn's glow spreading its circle of light about. The surface of the earth was freshened by morning breezes and moistened by tender showers. The stars dimmed as if falling asleep. Then the sun's bright orb rose, and the calm-rayed moon was rendered lustreless.

The herders and their cattle were already on the move. The road to Mathura was filled to overflowing. Cows walked ahead, followed by their calves guided with ropes by the herders. Behind came the bullocks hauling carts piled high with churns and other household gear. These slow carts were quickly left behind by the fast horse-drawn chariot in which Krishna and Balarama and Akrura rode. The three of them seated in Akrura's fine chariot looked as splendid as gods.

Later, when they had stopped to rest beside the Yamuna, Akrura said to Krishna, "Stay here, my boy, to tend the horses. Check over the harness and chariot while I am gone. And give the horses some fodder. They have been going hard and are weary and hungry. I plan to enter the Yamuna at this spot because they say it is where Ananta lives. I wish to see the blue-sheathed, double-tongued Ananta who bears the auspicious swastika on his head. If I worship this kindly snake from whose mouth flows a venom sweet as nectar, then I shall be at peace with all snakes. But I would like you two boys to stay here until I leave the presence of the serpent king."

Krishna agreed, adding, "Please come back soon. We don't wish to be separated from you for long."

Akrura dived down into the depths of the Yamuna, where he found the serpent realm. He first saw, in the center, the thousand-faced, lotus-eyed Vishnu, and then Vishnu in many of his separate forms. Vishnu thus also appeared as Balarama, the vanquisher of foes, with his palm-tree banner raised high. The

84

24. *Akrura Sees Krishna and Balarama in the Yamuna River*

full-grown Balarama was sprawled there in drunken slumber. His distinctive weapon, the plow, had slipped from his fingertips, and his club dangled disused across his belly. Pale-headed, pale-bodied, he was wrapped in dark blue garments and wore a single earring. He lay on a bed of serpent coils formed from his own body in his manifestation as Ananta, lord of serpents and of the undivided ocean. Balarama's golden crown tilted slightly to the left. His chest was garlanded with golden lotuses. Other lotuses were twined in his hair. His body was anointed with red sandalwood paste. Lotus-naveled, his body glowed like a white cloud from which glory flamed forth. Around him stood his serpent ministers, headed

85

by Vasuki. Two snake servants fanned him, others were bathing him with the waters of the undivided ocean poured from heavenly golden pitchers.

Akrura next saw yellow-garbed Vishnu seated on the coils of the snake Ananta. Vishnu's distinctive curl of hair was visible on his cloud-dark chest. Then Akrura saw, seated side by side, Krishna and Balarama. Having no divine thrones, they seemed to be merely the two splendid boys whom Akrura had left behind to tend his chariot. Akrura attempted to speak to Krishna there below the Yamuna, but Krishna with his glory rendered him speechless. Rising then up out of the water, Akrura was amazed to see still seated in his chariot the two wondrously formed youths, glancing calmly one at the other. Akrura excitedly dived down again into the Yamuna's depths. This time, he saw young Krishna seated on the vast coils of the serpent king Ananta and being worshiped with all the honor due the thousand-faced, eternal Vishnu.

After worshiping Krishna, so awesomely situated there, Akrura, his heart filled with praise, returned to his chariot, where the two boys were still seated. With a smile Krishna asked, "What was it like down there? You were gone so long, you must have seen something amazing."

Akrura replied, "Without you, what wonder could there be in all the worlds? Krishna, I saw there a sight so splendid, it is scarcely imaginable on earth. But I also see it here and I rejoice. Now let us be off, as the sun will be setting soon."

In Akrura's fast cart they easily reached Mathura by sundown. Akrura insisted that Krishna and Balarama stay with him in his own home and not go immediately to Vasudeva's house. "Because of Kamsa, that would only make more trouble for poor Vasudeva," Akrura cautioned anxiously.

"We shall certainly do as you wish," Krishna replied. "But since we have come by chance to the famous city of Mathura, we would like to see the sights." Akrura consented and gave them directions.

In the gathering dusk, the two brothers quickly set out, as excited as two young bull elephants straining at their posts and aching for a fight. Coming upon a man dyeing clothes, they wanted to acquire some of his freshly gleaming garments. But the dyer said angrily, "Where are you idiots from? These are for the king. I am coloring these expensive fabrics with rare and exotic dyes brought from various

25. *Krishna Kills the King's Dyer*

foreign lands expressly for King Kamsa. What jungle have you two been roaming about in all your lives? Maybe you're not bandits, but you certainly are not very bright if you think you can afford to buy clothes like these.''

Krishna was enraged. The dyer had been very foolish to antagonize him. With his lightning-like fist, Krishna struck him on the head. The dyer fell back, his head shattered. Seeing him dead, his wives set up an angry wail and, hair flying, fled away toward Kamsa's palace.

The two youths, now splendidly decked out in Kamsa's own clothes, decided they would also like some garlands. Guided as surely as two elephants following a sweet scent, they came upon a flower vendor named Gunaka, who had a pleasant face. His shop was hung with charming garlands. In a polite way Krishna asked if they might take some. "By all means," Gunaka replied at once. Even though he made his living selling flowers, he gave them his magnificent garlands unhesitatingly. "Bless you," Krishna exclaimed, and because he was pleased with Gunaka, he granted him a boon. "I shall use my power to make sure that you will always prosper," Krishna told him. Humbly bowing low, the flower merchant acknowledged Krishna's kindness. Actually, he was terrified because he thought they were supernatural Yakshas. He could not stammer a word of thanks.

Vasudeva's sons resumed their stroll through the main streets. They next encountered a hunchback woman laden with all sorts of precious pastes and oils. "Hunchback," Krishna said to her, "whose oils are these? Won't you tell me, Lotus-Eyes?"

The woman, whose eyes were beautiful but whose back was as curved as lightning, was charmed by this compliment from the lotus-eyed, cloud-dark Krishna and answered him eagerly. "Bless you for speaking so kindly to me," she said. "Would you like some of these oils? But first, tell me, where are you from that you did not recognize me? I was on my way to the royal baths. I am the king's personal masseuse."

Krishna replied, "We would love to have your oils because we are wrestlers who have come to take part in the king's athletic festival."

The hunchback was delighted. "Please take these," she said excitedly. "They were intended for the king." With her oils the brothers happily rubbed their splendid bodies until they glistened like two bulls emerging from the Yamuna all smeared with mud. Suddenly Krishna grasped her hump in his two skilled hands and pressed. He raised her body up as readily as if it had been a drooping vine. Realizing that her hump had disappeared and that her body was now flawless, she gasped for joy. She became like one possessed, maddened with love for Krishna. "Don't go!" she cried. "Darling, stay with me!" Krishna and Balarama exchanged embarrassed glances, because they had heard of the unflattering reputation of hunchback women. Krishna begged off, and they quickly fled from the aroused former hunchback.

Soon they reached the palace gates. The two boys from rural Vraja boldly entered the royal precincts, trying not to show any sign of hesitancy that might betray them. Confident as Himalayan lions, they made straight for the king's

26. *Krishna Raises up the Hunchback Maiden*

arsenal. Eager to see the archer's bow to which Kamsa had dedicated his athletic festival, they asked directions of an arsenal guard. Speaking politely, they said, "Listen, my good man. You, we know, are the worthy protector of King Kamsa's bows. Would you be so kind as to point out to us the bow to which the present festival is dedicated?"

Deferentially the guard took them to see it. Immediately seizing that gigantic bow stout as a post that even Indra could not string, Krishna lifted it up. Effortlessly brandishing about the awesome gem-encrusted bow, which was as elegantly curled as a snake, Krishna joyously hefted it up, strung it, and drew it so far back that it broke in two. Then Krishna sped away with Balarama right on his heels.

The bow's breaking made a sound like roaring wind. It rattled the inner

89

chambers of the palace and was heard for a great distance beyond. The horrified arsenal guard raced into Kamsa's presence and, panting with fear, he stammered, "An amazing thing has happened! Is the world coming to an end? There were these two young men. I never saw them before. They had bound-up hair, were wearing blue and yellow clothes, and were smeared with yellow and white pastes. Bright as fire, they seemed like young gods. All of a sudden, they were right in the arsenal as if dropped from the sky. I saw them perfectly, all hung with their gleaming garlands. One of them had lotus-shaped eyes. He was very dark, with yellow garlands. He took hold of that bow that even gods can't lift. This boy, I tell you, simply seized that bow that is like iron and strung it as easily as if it were a toy. Then he bent it with his big arms until it broke in the middle with a fearful cracking sound. After breaking that bow the way an elephant might snap a pole, he fled like the wind with the other one, I don't know where. I can't say who they were, O great King!" But Kamsa had heard all he needed to know. Dismissing the guard, he returned to his sumptuous private apartments in a distraught frame of mind.

Some time later, Kamsa paid a visit to the arena where the athletic festival would be held. There he saw everything arranged as befitted a proud monarch. Placed prominently in the stadium were row upon row of spectators' platforms, spacious, firmly set, with retiring rooms behind. Below Kamsa's own majestic platform were tented enclosures for the king's servants. And lining the arena were plain wooden benches, laced by numerous aisles, which could hold multitudes of ordinary spectators.

Reassured that the stadium was ready, Kamsa ordered that it now be decorated with garlands and many-colored flags. "Let awnings be strung above the platforms for important personages," he commanded, "and set roofs over the stalls. There should be plenty of cow dung for the arena floor, and bunting for the pillars. Bring lots of water in and fill all the golden pitchers to the brim. Place jars of scent about. Let the umpires be invited, and the guilds with their leaders. Let an order be given to the wrestlers to assemble, and instructions posted for the spectators." Having issued his commands, Kamsa, his confidence somewhat restored, left the elegant stadium and returned to the palace.

There he sent for Chanura and Mustika. These two enormously powerful huge-armed wrestlers were very much excited by the king's summons and responded quickly. After carefully assessing the two unbeaten wrestlers as they stood before him, Kamsa made them this proposition. "My good men," he said, "you are both superb athletes, far-famed for your physical prowess and well rewarded for it. When you recall the good treatment you have always received at my hands, you will not be surprised that I now have a serious assignment for you. There are two herders who live in one of my villages in Vraja. They are named Balarama and Krishna, still boys, actually, though strong. These country fellows are coming to Mathura to wrestle in the athletic festival. I want you to kill them. Do it quickly, but make it look like a ring accident. They say these two worthless youths are agile. By no means underestimate them. You will have to make an effort. But enough of this. Their destruction would serve me well. Need I say more?"

Chanura and Mustika loved fighting and cheerfully agreed to do as Kamsa wished. "As soon as we see those fellows, they are as good as dead," they asserted gruffly. "If those herder kids want a fight, we'll give them more than they bargained for!" The two wrestlers, big as bulls, were still shouting boastfully as they departed.

Kamsa next called in his elephant trainer. "Take that elephant named Kuvalayapida," Kamsa ordered, "and station him at the entrance to the stadium. As you know, that elephant is powerful and quick. His eyes dart about restlessly, and because he is rich in *mada* juice he can be easily aroused to fury against men. When you see Balarama and Krishna approaching the gate, set the elephant on them. I want those sons of Vasudeva destroyed. When Vasudeva and Devaki see their last sons slain and their whole line cut off, they will surely die. Then all those other idiot relatives of mine who have been chasing after Krishna will lose heart. It doesn't matter who kills those two, your elephant, the wrestlers, or you. So long as the city is rid of them, I shall be content. My kinsmen are all repudiating me, to take Krishna's side.

"You should know that I am not the son of that weakling Ugrasena. Narada explained it all to me: My mother once spent the day with her women in a delectable grove on the slope of the Suyamuna Hill. They enjoyed themselves there, strolling through the trees and by the streams, along the vales and crests. Heavenly musicians sang to her softly, and she listened delightedly. Peacocks called,

91

small birds warbled, sounding especially sweet to her that day for she was in her fertile period. Breezes whispered through the trees. The wind bore an ever-strengthening scent of Kadamba, whose fragrant orange blossoms, glistening like lamps, wakened thoughts of love. Petals drifting down like rain urged her further. The earth seemed like a reclining maiden coyly draped in a bright garment of new grass twinkling with red beetles.

"Just then, the demon Drumila came there disguised as Ugrasena. My mother eagerly yielded herself. But as they lay together his strength betrayed him. She started up frightened and said, 'You are certainly not my husband! Who do you think you are to sully my honor? You have treacherously ruined a virtuous woman. What will my in-laws say when they learn I have disgraced their family? They will say I am nothing but a whore! Shame, shame, you lustful family-defiler!'

"Angered by her words, the demon replied, 'Woman, I am Drumila, ruler of the celestial city of Saubha. Why do you stupidly blame me for taking the place of your feeble husband? Women are not sullied by infidelity. What woman would deny me? Most mortal women would do anything to gain a godlike son. Why are you so vain of your virtue, tossing your head back grandly? I tell you, I have just given you a son. His name will be Kamsa, and he will be a terror to his foes.'

"My mother became even angrier at this and said, 'Now you have insulted all honest wives! I know that some women are wanton, but others are faithful. Have you never heard of Arundhati, the patroness of conjugal fidelity? The three worlds are upheld by faithful women who reverence Arundhati. As for this son you say you have given me, I am not impressed by this so-called boon. I would rather have my good name back. Do you know what has been foretold? The imperishable one is destined to take birth in my husband's family. He will be the death of this son of yours, Vow-destroyer!'

"When she had finished, Drumila left for his sky city, and my poor mother returned home carrying me in her womb. So you see, Elephant-trainer, I am only ostensibly Ugrasena's son. Rejected by both my father and my mother, I have established myself by my own prowess. I am hated by my parents, indeed by all my clansmen. I shall kill them all, once these herders are put away.

"Go get your sharpest goads and weapons. Mount that elephant and station yourself at the arena gate. You must not fail me!"

❊❦ VII ❦❊

In the Arena

EAGER spectators jammed the awesome arena. With their movement and sounds, the multitudes of people filling that immoveable structure gave it the appearance of a rolling sea. The benches for the thousands of ordinary spectators were of plain wood, solidly made. But the freestanding platforms occupied by the most important spectators were ornately embellished with octagonal columns, exquisitely carved half-moon-shaped windows, and stout doors. Colorfully bedecked with bright fabrics, with ropes of tastefully fashioned flowers strung along their sides, these platforms were as colorful as autumn clouds floating above the moving ocean. With their bright turrets adorned with yak tails fluttering in the wind, and with glittering festoons and flapping curtains, these high platforms resembled winged mountains in the sky. Many of these cleverly constructed platforms were occupied by guilds of artisans and professional associations. Each of these sported the banner of its particular trade.

Not far away were the stands for the women of the royal household. These pavilions gleamed with gold and shining gems. Public courtesans occupied separate stands, which were decorated with fine fabrics. These pavilions with their elegant occupants had the splendor of heavenly palaces. They were decorated with gold, lined with colorful carpets, and furnished with vases of flowers. Golden pitchers of wine and platters of fruit and sorrel-flavored snacks glimmered in the foyers.

Modest women were also provided for. They could observe the festivities through pierced screens from rooms in the arena's towers, arrayed so high overhead they resembled soaring geese.

Set prominently forward, as dominant in the arena as Mount Meru surrounded by foothills, stood Kamsa's own empty platform, with its columns ornamented with splendidly worked gold leaf. Heavily draped with garlands of flowers, it seemed endowed with every royal attribute. All but the king were in their places. Then, after making sure that the elephant Kuvalayapida was stationed at the gate, Kamsa entered the arena. Resplendent in white garments, wearing a white crown and fanned by white yak tails, he glowed like the moon wreathed in pale clouds. As the king seated himself on his majestic lion throne, the vast crowd, awed by his splendor, hailed him loudly. Then the wrestlers entered, their robes fluttering in the breeze, and stood around three sides of the central space.

Balarama and Krishna heard the fanfares welling from the arena and excitedly approached the gate. But as the two youths ran up, they found their way blocked by Kuvalayapida. Goaded forward by his trainer, the maddened elephant, coiling his snakelike trunk, furiously assaulted the two heroes. Krishna smiled grimly as he watched the maddened elephant bearing down. "This is surely Kamsa's doing," he thought. "He is trying to destroy me by setting this elephant on me, but he is the one who will soon be dead."

As the elephant rushed forward, Krishna leapt into the air and clapped his hands. Kuvalayapida tried repeatedly to wrap his trunk about Krishna's chest, but time after time Krishna eluded him by bounding up between his tusks or darting through his legs. Krishna chased over and under him like a breeze buffeting a cloud. The elephant could not get at Krishna with his head, his trunk, his tusks, or his legs. Krishna dealt with that elephant as if it were a child's plaything. Finally, bewildered by his inability to crush Krishna, the huge-bodied beast fell forward on his knees, bellowing in anguish. He drove his tusks into the earth and his *mada* juice flowed out like rain from a monsoon cloud at the end of the hot season. Then, placing his foot on Kuvalayapida's head, Krishna uprooted one of his tusks and struck him in the face with it. The elephant, pierced by his own thunderbolt-like tusk, roared with pain, releasing urine and excrement in his fright. Blood gushed from his shattered temples. Then Balarama, looking like the bird Garuda tugging at a snake half-hidden under a rock, dragged the hulking corpse to one side by the tail.

Krishna had killed that mighty beast with one blow of his own tusk. Kuvalayapida had tumbled down like a mountain split by lightning, bringing his trainer along with him. After rendering that great tusker tuskless, Krishna strode on with Balarama into the packed, ocean-like arena. The two youths bounded in rapidly, their garments flowing out behind. Krishna was a frightening sight because his body was smeared with the *mada* juice and blood of the elephant whose tusk he

94

27. *Krishna Eludes the Elephant Demon Kuvalayapida*

still held. Leaping like a lion, roaring like a cloud, he shook the earth when he slapped his upper arms. Seeing Krishna prancing about holding high Kuvalaya-pida's uprooted tusk, Kamsa trembled with rage. Brandishing that curving tusk in his hand, Krishna resembled a hill with a new moon rising over it. As he leapt around the ring, the excited spectators roared their approval.

At a signal from Kamsa, Chanura, red-eyed with rage, rushed into the center of the ring to challenge Krishna. Though warned by Kamsa to be cautious, instead he danced forward furiously like a cloud frantic to discharge its water. The match was announced and the crowd fell silent. But some of Kamsa's kinsmen protested. "The rules regulating wrestling are long established," they insisted. "Wrestling is a trial of skill and strength, not an armed brawl. If two contestants are considered well matched, they are daubed with cow dung, and the judges will then direct whether they should start standing up or on the ground. No wrestler is ever permitted to oppose someone of a different age and weight, because that is the only way to prevent fatal accidents. How can the king authorize a bout between Krishna and Chanura when Krishna is still a youth and Chanura is a full-grown giant of a man?''

The whole arena was buzzing with argument. Then Krishna came forward. "It is true," he said, "I am a boy and Chanura is built like a mountain. I want to wrestle him anyway. On my side, there will be no violation of the rules of combat. The usual preliminaries—washing, cow-dung daubing and so forth—will be gone through as is prescribed for wrestlers. But once it starts, I warn you this fight will be no ordinary wrestling bout. If I win, the world will rejoice, because Chanura in past years has killed many opponents in his wild rages. Hoping to make a fine name for himself, he has instead given wrestling a bad name. Wrestling is not like war. A death in battle gives the victor lasting glory and his victim a place in heaven. Such a death is honorable for both slayer and slain. But does a wrestling victim go to heaven? What true sportsman would take pleasure in killing his opponent? And a king who encourages wrestling to the death because he thinks this will enhance his fame is as contemptible as the killer in the ring!"

The people jamming the arena began cheering unrestrainedly, those occupying the raised seats of honor as much as all the rest. Kamsa reacted sullenly as it became evident that they were all cheering for Krishna. Sweat poured down his face, and with his left hand he signaled the trumpeters to refrain from a fanfare. But overhead drums and trumpets could be heard played by heavenly musicians accompanying the gods who hovered over the arena in their divine chariots. "Krishna," they called out, "defeat the demon Chanura!"

Chanura and Krishna fought like two wild elephants. They tangled together, legs and arms flying, pounding away as if determined to grind each other up. Shaking and snorting like wild boars, they gouged with their fists, elbows, and fingernails, they kicked each other savagely, they dug their knees into each other's sides. That was what this so-called sporting bout was like.

Krishna struggled with Chanura for a very long time. At last Chanura began to weaken, and Krishna hurled him to the ground. From the force of his fall, the arena seats shook and the finest gem dropped from Kamsa's crown. Chanura bounded up, but again Krishna threw him down, this time also smashing Chanura's head with his fist and crushing a knee into Chanura's chest. Chanura's eyes were driven from their sockets and hung down covered with tears and blood like little golden bells rimming an elephant's girth. Proud of his strength, Chanura had been reckless. Now his lifeless body loomed like a mountain in the huge arena.

After Chanura fell, Mustika rushed out. Balarama struggled with him for a time as they rolled and twisted about. Then with one thundering blow of his powerful fist, Balarama shattered his skull the way lightning rends a mountain. His brains spilled out, his eyes fell out. Then Krishna and Balarama, their eyes flashing with triumphant rage, leapt to the center of the arena. The crowd sent up a great roar hailing the deaths of Chanura and Mustika at the hands of Krishna and Balarama. Seeing their comrades' fate, all the king's remaining wrestlers fled.

Nanda and the other Vrindavana herders had been watching, trembling with fear in every limb. Devaki too had been shaking with fear, but now her eyes filled with joyous tears. Vasudeva's eyes were also dimmed with loving tears as he witnessed the triumph of his sons. He felt young again.

Like bees hovering around a flower, elegant courtesans in their fine pavilions were darting fond glances at Krishna's lotus face. But sweat beaded Kamsa's brow. His mind was darkened by his desire for Krishna's death as black smoke fanned by an angry wind obscures a fire's light. His lips were trembling, his forehead furrowed. His angry face, red and sweating, resembled the rising sun. He turned to his bodyguards and shouted, "Get those two jungle herders out of here! I don't ever want to see them again. Throw them out of my country, and all those other cowherds too! Make sure not one of them is left. That idiot Nanda has persistently opposed me. Get him with your iron fetters. Vasudeva deceived me. Quick, kill him! Don't spare your clubs because his hair is white. And seize the cows and everything else those herders have."

As Kamsa raged, Krishna stood silent. He watched calmly as Devaki fainted and Vasudeva and Nanda and his herder friends were imperiled. Then with one lion-like leap, all-conquering Krishna bounded up from the arena floor toward Kamsa's high seat. Like lightning flashing from cloud to cloud, he rose so fast no one saw his leap. The spectators below simply saw him standing beside Kamsa, and Kamsa thought Krishna had dropped from the sky. Taking Kamsa's hair in an iron grip, Krishna dragged him down into the dirt. His diamond-studded crown crashed to one side. Held by the hair, gasping for breath, Kamsa could not see his tormentor's face. The king's mind was deranged, his body disfigured as Krishna

28. *Krishna Drags King Kamsa from His Throne*

plowed a trench across the arena with Kamsa's body and then tossed the lifeless corpse to one side. No earrings gleamed now in his ears, no necklaces adorned his chest. Every limb was stripped of ornament. Dragged down by the hair from his high throne, his white clothes scraped away, the once resplendent king had become a dingy heap of flesh. His eyes were sightless, his face blackened, his crown gone. In death he had become as dismal as a lotus with its petals stripped away. Kamsa had not fallen valorously in battle from an enemy's arrows. His scratched and gouged corpse seemed to have been clawed to death.

Between them Balarama and Krishna had dispatched every foe, because Balarama had crushed Kamsa's villainous brother to death with his bare hands. The two brothers who had so long lived hidden in Vraja had freed Mathura completely from Kamsa's thrall.

Seeming now doubly luminous with joy, lotus-eyed Krishna, his enemy destroyed, went to greet his parents. He bowed to his father and pressed his head against his mother's feet. Devaki's blissful tears caressed his head. Glowing with power, Krishna then greeted all his other kinsmen in order of rank and age.

29. *Krishna's Heroic Deeds in the City of Mathura*

❧ VIII ❧

A Time for Healing

SEEING their husband slain, Kamsa's wives came and flocked around his corpse like does mourning a fallen buck. "Our great-armed lord is gone," they wept, "and we are left without friends or hope. Our roots have been cut. Who will gratify us when our limbs tremble with desire like vines shaken by the wind? You were always fond of earrings, and now your ears are bare. Where is the jeweled crown that shone like the sun above your head? The sun burns down on your tender face as cruelly as on a lotus out of water.

"Lord, when you confronted your foes, you always seemed the equal of Death. We thought we needed no protection but yours. Now you have been thrown down by Death and we are left with a miserable widow's life, with nothing to do but weep. Lord, you taught us only pleasure, not how to bear this pain. How can women accustomed to a palace learn to live drearily? We sighed only to loll in your arms, but in an instant you are gone! Because of one man's crimes we are all made widows. After lulling us with heavenly pleasures, making us slaves to your love, now where have you gone? We are here, Lord, wailing like ospreys! Why won't you answer us?

"O great King, your going is cruel payment to loyal wives and friends. Are the women in that other world more beautiful? Is that why you left us? Here we are, making this great lamentation, and still you ignore us! Should a man so blithely leave his wives? Women with no husband are more fortunate than the wives of a hero. Heroes dream of courting the women of paradise because those women like heroes. Now Death has seized our glory-hungry lord and what are we to do?

"When Indra tried to withhold his rains, you punctured his clouds with your arrows. With your shafts you shook the unshakeable sea and stole the sea god Varuna's gems. Unconquerable even by these gods, how could you have been slain by a mortal? Every earthly king stood in awe of your power, offering you

101

tributes of cloth-and precious jewels. Your enemies all feared your godlike strength. How could you have suffered such a death as this?

"Lord, we lie helpless at your feet. Please come back from that much-too-distant land. Could you not at least have said 'I will be going'? How can you bear to lie there in the dust? Aren't you uncomfortable? Of all women, surely we are the most ill-used. All we have left of life is grief."

They were still weeping when Kamsa's mother, frail and trembling, came there from the palace. "Where is my child? Where is my boy?" she cried frantically. Seeing her slain son, his body darkened like the moon in eclipse, she exclaimed, "Oh! Anything but this!" Then she dropped to the ground and placed her son's wretched head in her lap. In a voice quavering with grief she said softly, "My dear child, you were always brave, always the delight of my heart. Why have you left me? Must you go? It is not right that you should lie on the bare ground. What will become of us all? Before he was slain by Rama, the demon king Ravana told his kinsmen, 'Mighty as I seem, a vanquisher of gods, even I can be destroyed by my own kin.' So it has proved for my son."

Steadying herself, the old queen turned to her bewildered husband, Ugrasena. "See your royal son lying here like a lightning-struck hill," she said. "He is dead and we should attend to his last rites. But first you must ask Krishna's permission. Victors rule in this life. He may not object. What offense can a dead man give?"

Tearing her hair in grief, the queen gazed down sorrowfully again like a cow beside her dead calf. "My child," she mourned, "what will your wives do now? Accustomed to ease, believing themselves fortunate in having such a husband, now they see every hope dashed. And must I watch my husband wither under Krishna's eye like shallow water drying up? My son, I am your mother! Why don't you answer? You left on this journey without warning. Death seized you and took this poor old woman unaware. All those you gratified, on whom you showered honors and wealth, your servants and retainers, all now mourn their lord's death. Please rise, my fine long-armed son, and help these people who need you." Kamsa's mother and wives were still there when the sun's rays reddened into evening.

Sorrowful old Ugrasena, feeling as unsteady as a man who has just drunk poison, had meanwhile gone to seek out Krishna. He found Krishna seated at home surrounded by his kinsmen, regretfully meditating on the calamity he had

30. Kamsa's Household Mourns His Death

caused Kamsa's household. Moved by the anguish of Kamsa's mother and wives, Krishna spoke apologetically. "I killed Kamsa, I fear, with a young man's recklessness," he told his assembled kinsmen. "In my rage I forgot that this deed would widow Kamsa's thousand wives. Death himself was surely saddened by their outpouring of grief. My thoughts beforehand, I confess, were of Kamsa.

"I killed Kamsa because he lived only for evil. The quiet of death, I thought, was preferable to the activeness of life for a ruler whose methods were low, whose understanding was weak and whose temper was cruel. Kamsa was condemned by just persons and disliked by everyone. What pity could he inspire? A good ruler gains paradise after death as fulfillment for his deeds and even in this life may gain fame. But a bad ruler makes virtuous action difficult for everyone. Only

31. *Krishna Restores Ugrasena as King of Mathura*

Death can salvage justice then. When I killed Kamsa, the damage done by his misrule was ended. Let his family seek consolation in this thought. And let the people of the city take heart."

Ugrasena bowed his head, grieved to recollect his son's misdeeds. His voice was choked with tears as he answered Krishna. "My son," he said, "you have banished anger from our land. May your name be ever praised as the restorer of righteousness. Your worth has long been known to good people. Now all your enemies have been made anxious. You have raised up your friends and made your allies proud. Neighboring rulers will hear of your deeds and be eager to befriend you. Ordinary people will follow you, priests will extol you, ministers will vie to advise you about war and peace. Kamsa's army with all its elephants, horses, chariots, and regiments of foot soldiers is yours to command. Your friends can help themselves to our money, our grain, our jewels, our cloth, our women, our gold, and whatever else of value they may choose.

"You have triumphed, Krishna. This country is yours to rule. Please, I have only one request, that I may perform Kamsa's last rites, now that his evil deeds have been consumed by the fire of your wrath. If I am permitted this, I shall then take my wife and daughters-in-law to the forest and wander there among the wild beasts. Our family's obligations will have been discharged once Kamsa's rites are performed correctly. Please show mercy and grant a poor old man's request."

Krishna was moved by Ugrasena's plea and replied consolingly. "How could I oppose so natural a wish? Let Kamsa be cremated properly so that his soul may find rest. I will give the orders.

"I assure you," Krishna continued, "I did not throw down Kamsa to gain his throne. The credit of having helped this country is all I seek. I have always lived among cows and cowherds. I love roaming as much as a wild elephant. That life is a hundred times better than one of royal luxury. I tell you truthfully, I do not crave a king's crown. Ugrasena, I consider you foremost among the nobles of Mathura. You should again be consecrated king of this land. If you wish to please me and it does not vex you, take back your former throne."

Ugrasena stood abashed and humbled as Krishna in the presence of the assembled nobles of Mathura gave instructions for his consecration. When the crown had been placed once more on his head, Ugrasena together with Krishna made arrangements for Kamsa's cremation. Responsive to Krishna's desire, the nobles of Mathura followed King Ugrasena as readily as the Thirty Gods follow Indra.

Under a brilliant sun his kinsmen bore Kamsa's body in state to the northern bank of the Yamuna, where his funeral pyre was ignited. Kamsa's brother was cremated alongside. When these ceremonies were completed, they all returned with Ugrasena in the lead to Mathura.

Detail of Gate Posts at Mandor (See page 108)

POSTSCRIPT
THE ILLUSTRATIONS

Indian tradition determinedly unites the arts, in the belief that aesthetic understanding is best furthered by a combination of sensory stimuli. This belief is superbly reflected in several great manuscripts, from which come most of the paintings reproduced in this book. I have attempted to follow Indian tradition to some extent by arranging these paintings as they were originally arranged, in narrative sequence, rather than by region or date. Indian manuscript illustrations are not simply artifacts or objects of beauty. They still nourish a living tradition. By encountering the paintings while simultaneously encountering the *Harivamsa*'s story, one may perhaps begin to experience them in the way initially intended.

The tradition of Krishna representation is extremely old. What is probably the earliest surviving portrayal of a recognizable series of incidents from Krishna's life dates from the fourth century A.D. and consists of two gate posts from Mandor in Rajasthan (see illustration, page 108). The custom of representing the Krishna story was undoubtedly established even earlier, indeed as soon as the story itself took shape. Beginning with the fourth century, a continuous tradition of narrative Krishna representation in stone and bronze can readily be traced, a tradition augmented from the fifteenth century forward by surviving manuscript paintings. Sculpture and painting stem from a single iconographic tradition. Motifs found in early sculpture are regularly utilized in later manuscript illustrations, often with astonishing exactitude. Krishna's fight with Keshin as represented in the fourth century at Mandor, for example (illustration, page 108, lower left), is quite similar in conception to a depiction of that same incident painted more than a thousand years later (figure 23).

Like any living entity, the Indian tradition has nonetheless evolved. Changes can be traced not simply in style but also in basic conceptions. Thus, in the early *Harivamsa* version of the story, as in the Mandor sculpture (illustration, page 108, upper right), Krishna holds up the Govardhana Hill in the palm of his hand. In most later versions, Krishna is described and shown holding Govardhana on the tip of his little finger (figure 17). In the *Harivamsa*, similarly, Krishna's uprooting

107

Gate Posts at Mandor. Photographed in their original location in 1909, these posts were subsequently removed from Mandor to the Jodhpur Museum, a few miles away.

The episodes depicted on the left-hand post from top to bottom are: Balarama watching Dhenuka fall from a palmyra tree; Krishna placing one foot on Kaliya's head; Pralamba carrying off Balarama; Krishna killing Arishta; and Krishna killing Keshin. On the right-hand post from top to bottom can be seen Krishna holding the Govardhana Hill in his palm while cows look on below; Krishna stealing butter as Yasoda scolds; and Krishna overturning the cart. A lintel probably once connected the two posts, but one can only speculate concerning what additional scene or scenes it might have displayed.

of the two old trees is purely and simply a catastrophe, indicating the infant Krishna's strength but nothing more. In later versions, pious chroniclers devised a purpose for Krishna's randomly destructive act, the liberation of two persons trapped inside the trees (figure 8). The *Harivamsa*'s account, moreover, reeks of real stableyards, whereas many later paintings and poems transform the herders' homely campground in Vrindavana into a marble-pavilioned pleasure garden, literally heaven on earth. The tendency of the tradition, in other words, has been to make Krishna more "astonishing" and more continually didactic, and to transform the rustic realism of the *Harivamsa*'s suspenseful account of the gradual revelation of Krishna's nature and mission into something more resembling a grand progress through life. But even when weighted down by piety or princely attire, Krishna usually manages to radiate his special kind of energy.

Some Krishna paintings survive from before 1500 A.D., but the great era of Krishna painting, as of Indian miniature painting generally, extends from the sixteenth to the early nineteenth century. Coinciding with an intensification of religious devotion to Krishna, this important era of artistic activity began in the sixteenth century with an explosion of creative vitality. Manuscript illustrators, now painting on fine handmade paper in a larger format than had been permitted by narrow palm leaf strips, experimented with a number of new techniques.

One manuscript in particular must have done much to spur this new boldness. An illustrated manuscript of the *Bhagavata Purana*, it is sometimes referred to as the Mita Ram-Nana manuscript because either the name Mita Ram or the name Nana appears on a great many of the paintings. Some scholars have speculated that Mita Ram and Nana were the names of two artists, but others have suggested that Mita Ram and Nana were once joint owners of the manuscript and informally divided it between themselves. This manuscript (represented here by figures 2, 6, 12, 14, 15, 18 and 27) may have originally contained as many as two hundred paintings by various artists. Sometimes these painters appear to be dealing almost playfully with their inherited tradition. The rigid boxes into which paintings had ordinarily been fitted in the long, thin "comic-strip" style of palm leaf manuscripts are broken apart and recombined. Borders become platforms to stand on or posts to lean against as these old constraints are incorporated inventively into the action. The painters of the Mita Ram-Nana manuscript also employed color in new ways. An interesting example is the spotlight effect created by the yellow space surrounding the demon elephant in figure 27. Such bright blocks of color boldly focus attention and set a mood. In these paintings color becomes itself a dramatic force.

Manuscripts illustrated several decades later reflect slightly different qualities. Paintings more frequently fill out a single rectangular space and evince a greater concern with realistic representation. One set of these later paintings, believed to have been done about 1570 A.D., comes from Isarda, near Jaipur in Rajasthan (see figures 4, 25, 26 and 31). Less startling than the Mita Ram-Nana series, this manuscript is also more romantic and refined. A lyrical quality is achieved by the rhythmic repetition of elegant forms, whose strong stylization is full of liveliness. In figure 4, for example, the two guards, their two shields, and the two dogs contribute to a magically restrained and balanced feeling. In figure 26 the parallel stances of the herders watching awestruck as Krishna raises up the stooped hunchback suggest the radiating circles of impact of this miracle across the world. By contrast, when the Mita Ram-Nana painters employed rhythmic repetition (see, for example, the leaping deer and boars of figure 15 or the wives of Kaliya in figure 12), they seem to have striven more for a sense of pulsating energy than of balance.

One area of especially sharp contrast between the earlier Mita Ram-Nana and the later Isarda paintings is the depiction of water. The omnipresent "basket-weave" motif for water of the Mita Ram-Nana manuscript (seen here in figures 6, 12 and 27) is replaced in the Isarda paintings by randomly swirling lines, as in figure 25. Some have suggested that this shift reflects the influence of the new naturalism fostered at the Mughal court under the Emperor Akbar, who ruled India from 1556 A.D. to 1605 A.D. Certainly the river shown in figure 25 does seem similar in some respects to the river created by Akbar's artist in figure 28. Yet, despite their drift toward naturalism and away from the summary abruptness of the Mita Ram-Nana paintings, the Isarda paintings contain no conclusive evidence of non-Hindu influence. By the last decades of the sixteenth century, however, Akbar had radically altered the character of Indian painting.

A Muslim ruler the majority of whose subjects were Hindus, Akbar felt strongly motivated to promote understanding between these often antagonistic faiths. Akbar assumed that most religious conflicts were caused by bigoted priestly classes with a vested interest in restricting popular access to knowledge of the positive merits of other faiths. Akbar hoped, in consequence, that by calling attention to ancient Krishna texts he could circumvent contemporary Hindu dogmatists and simultaneously neutralize ill-informed Muslim criticism of Krishna's followers. So Akbar ordered his scholars and painters to translate into Persian and to illustrate the ancient *Mahabharata* and the almost equally ancient *Harivamsa* rather than later Krishna texts of a more esoteric and devotional character, such as the *Gita Govinda* and *Bhagavata Purana,* then popular at Hindu courts. In Hinduism's vigorous early narratives of adventure, Akbar had found a Krishna he could wholeheartedly admire.

The Krishna portrayed in Akbar's manuscript of the *Harivamsa* (figures 10, 13 and 28) is an energetic political leader, the gallant protector of a fortunate people. This Krishna is depicted, appropriately enough, with an elaborate concern for social contexts. Using illusionistic techniques newly imported from Renaissance Europe, including vanishing-point depth perspective and the suggestion of volume by modeling, Akbar's painters offered a complete account of the setting of each of Krishna and Balarama's heroic deeds. Crowds of people are shown swirling about the center of attention, and frequently the viewer is led beyond both the central action and the masses of spectators to distant corners where animals and people unconcernedly go about their affairs (see, for example, figure 10).

In the hands of Akbar's painters, color becomes primarily an aesthetic accent rather than a mode of expression. Symbolic and theological levels of meaning are subordinated to a commitment to realism. It is interesting in this connection to contrast the demon elephant of figure 27, done by an artist working in the Hindu tradition, with the demon elephant of figure 28, painted for Akbar a few decades later. Summary expressiveness and bold, flat color accents now have been replaced by an infinitely subtle, ornate realism. The Akbar elephant's hide, for example, is carefully rendered with muted pinks and grays, and the portrayal of the elephant's housing has become an occasion for a virtuosic blue and gold ornamental display. Like their imperial master, Akbar's court artists knew how to combine opulence and refinement with boundless vitality.

Akbar's stylistic innovations left a permanent mark on Indian painting. Naturalistic elements were increasingly accepted by Hindu artists and blended with the older tradition of symbolic representation. A manuscript illustrated at the Hindu court of Bundi about 1640 A.D., a generation after Akbar's death, indicates the strength of Akbar's influence. The vertical format of these impressively large paintings is very similar to that of Akbar's *Harivamsa* and in their treatment of architecture and landscape the Bundi paintings often echo Mughal conventions. By showing many figures arrayed in a naturalistic landscape or courtyard, they also accord to the Krishna story some of the secular grandness of Akbar's own conception. Also, the demons of the Bundi manuscript are relatively earthbound. But in spirit the Bundi paintings are thoroughly distinct. The bold simplification of their design makes them more immediately comprehensible than Akbar's complicated compositions, and strong facial expressiveness gives them an engagingly bucolic openness. This permits more straightforward use of supernatural motifs, as is evident in the graceful directness of the Bundi representation of the lifting of the Govardhana Hill (figure 17).

In the paintings created in the late eighteenth century in the Hindu states of the Himalayan foothills (see figures 7, 9, 11, 19 and 24), even stronger naturalistic influences are apparent in the treatment of landscape and figures. But in these paintings as well, symbolism and stylization are evident. Figures 9 and 10 are, for example, both attempts to depict the realities of herder life. But Akbar's artist seems content simply to show a scene of bustling activity. The Kangra artist, while no less interested in lively detail, is at the same time as fascinated by parallel forms as were the painters of the Mita Ram-Nana and Isarda manuscripts.

Despite the powerful influence exerted by Akbar's naturalism, the Hindu tradition retained its visionary character. Indeed many post-Akbar schools of painting disdained naturalism almost entirely. A comparison of the animals in a pre-Akbar painting such as figure 15 with those in a post-Akbar painting such as figure 20 reveals just how vital the tradition of bold, flat stylization remained.

Because they are closer to Western sensibilities, Akbar's paintings are easier for most Westerners to respond to. But because they are closer to their subject, paintings done for Hindu patrons can sometimes offer greater insight into the meaning of the Krishna story. Akbar's painters were supremely skilled at producing good likenesses of human beings, animals, and vegetation. In contrast, the manipulation of shapes in Hindu art can seem strangely arbitrary. Forms are stretched about with complete plasticity. Women's breasts may be shaped like mangoes, as in figure 7; the legs of women and men may be made straight as tree trunks, as in figure 17; their arms elongated into tendril-like shapes, as in figure 12; or their hands molded to resemble flower buds, as in figure 20. Knees and elbows and fingers are usually drawn with flowing, continuous lines smoothing over the bony structures that Mughal and Western artists often take pride in accentuating. A person unfamiliar with Hindu aesthetics might be inclined to call the treatment of wrists, knees, and ankles in figure 26 the work of an inexperienced artist. In fact, this painting is a highly sophisticated attempt to suggest analogies to vegetative life.

If a modern Western poet were to compare a woman's arms to vines, the image might well seem farfetched. Because of the way the Western tradition distinguishes human beings from the rest of the created universe, a Western poet would have to be unusually clever to make effective use of such an image. In ancient India poets did not have to contend with this barrier. The emotional inclination felt by all people to find sympathy and kinship between different kinds of living things was nurtured and encouraged. Excellence in one mode of being seemed normally associated with excellence in other modes, so that a beautiful eye could sensibly be said and shown to resemble a beautiful flower petal.

Similarities in appearance hint of similarities in quality. Balarama, for example, is described as moon-colored. It is thus not surprising that he should turn out to have a touch of lunar lunacy. He temporarily forgets himself when carried off by Pralamba, until reminded of his powers by the ever-poised Krishna. And in later life Balarama develops a riotous capacity for indulgence, which is why the *Harivamsa* describes Akrura in his underwater vision as seeing the mature Balarama sprawled in a drunken stupor (see page 85).

Krishna, on the other hand, is dark-skinned as his name implies, because the Sanskrit word *krishna* literally means "dark" or "black." *Syama*, another word often used to describe Krishna, has the same connotations. One other adjective commonly applied to Krishna, *nil*, can be translated by the English color word "blue." More precisely, *nil* comprehends a range of hues from black to dark blue to slate gray. It can be described most simply as the color of a rain cloud. It is thus no surprise to hear that Krishna has the bounding energy of a brimming rain cloud.

Many persons in India have what could be called moon-colored skins; many others have *nil*-colored skins. Akbar's painters typically used approximations of these natural Indian skin colors for Balarama and Krishna (see, for example, figure 13). Painters working in a Mughal-influenced Hindu context have often used this same range of hues (see, for example, figures 16 and 17). But frequently in Hindu painting one encounters a very unmoonlike chalky white Balarama, and an equally uncloudlike sky-blue Krishna (see, for example, figures 26 and 27). Here color is used not simply to illustrate the poet's descriptive words but also to underscore a philosophic point. Such explicitly extraordinary skin colors separate Balarama and Krishna from the other persons depicted, who are usually shown with brown or gold skin tones. In addition, the use of bright blue and white emphasizes the relationship of complementarity that links the two divine brothers. Krishna and Balarama are contrasting aspects of an underlying unity, both being manifestations of Vishnu, the energizer of the universe.

The characteristic Hindu approach to artistic representation of the Krishna story is perhaps most broadly distinguishable from Akbar's by a quality of reverent intimacy. In contrast to the densely populated vistas Akbar preferred, Hindu paintings ordinarily have a quality of focused intimacy emblematic of their intended use as aids to personal devotion. Even when representing battles or royal courts, these paintings seem intensely private. In figure 29, for example, we are given an overall view of the city of Mathura, with numerous people busily engaged in a variety of activities. But instead of a single center of action, we find several, intended to be encountered in sequence in a series of mounting steps. Even the dramatic climax, the toppling of Kamsa, is depicted as an event occurring in the absence of all spectators. Krishna's presence has not transformed the city in the way envisioned by Akbar's painter in figure 28. In the Hindu version, Krishna is seemingly present everywhere at once, directly encountering individuals face to face.

Hindu painting may be said to strive ordinarily for a stirring immediacy of relationship between the viewer and the subject represented. Not being confined to a specific setting, Krishna becomes more directly available to the viewer, ready, in effect, to step right out of the picture. Hindu paintings seem ultimately designed to pull the viewer away from all contexts into a mystical union with a timeless, placeless Krishna. At their best they succeed in conveying simultaneously Krishna's awesome supernatural power and his human approachability. Krishna in these paintings both terrifies and charms. He is both a transcendent god and a member of the family. He is so close that we boldly reach out to touch him as a friend or lover, and so startling that we respond immediately when he asks us to do the most unconventional things.

In the following pages, these reflections on the historical development and objectives of Indian paintings of the Krishna theme are supplemented through separate analyses of each of the paintings reproduced in the text.

1. The Earth-Cow Flees King Parthu

Basohli, c.1765 A.D. *Museum of Fine Arts, Boston. 180 x 280 mm. Reproduced in Milo C. Beach, "A* Bhagavata Purana *from the Punjab Hills,"* Bulletin, *Museum of Fine Arts, Boston, lxiii (1965), p. 168.*

Sensing that flight is hopeless, the Earth-Cow turns back to consider making an appeal for mercy to the king. King Parthu is a grand and vigorous ruler. But the Earth-Cow serenely dominates this painting, as she will soon conquer the heart of the king. Milk-white, nimble, of noble proportions, she seems entirely capable of leaping effortlessly into the heavens or of launching into a persuasive discourse.

This painting is from what W. G. Archer labeled the "sixth" Basohli *Bhagavata* series, a series closely related in style to the slightly earlier "fifth" series, from which comes figure 16. For Archer's discussion of both series, see his *Indian Paintings from the Punjab Hills,* London: Sotheby, 1973, ii, 49ff.

2. Brahma, Shiva, Indra, a Herder, and the Earth-Cow Ask the Unseen Vishnu to Manifest Himself on Earth

North India, c.1540 A.D. *From the same manuscript as figures 6, 12, 14, 15, 18 and 27. The Kronos Collections. 175 x 230 mm.*

Followers of Vishnu believe that the eternal Vishnu first created Brahma, who then created the other gods. Brahma is therefore sometimes called "Grandfather" and here is shown as a portly, four-headed, white-bearded dignitary. A much more youthful-looking Shiva carries a trident, wears a tigerskin and is surmounted by a white cobra. He has a third eye in the middle of his forehead and a blue neck, acquired when he swallowed a world-menacing poison that appeared when the gods and demons churned the ocean for *amarta* (see pages 15, 73). Shiva's long black hair, in which he caught the Ganges when it fell suddenly from heaven, reaches almost to his knees. "Thousand-eyed" Indra is shown with only six extra eyes, since the artist's preference is for very large eyes. Indra is seemingly middle-aged, in keeping with his role as the heavenly model of earthly kingship. A boyish herder attends the Earth-Cow, whose prominent ribs and shrunken udder symbolize the distress that only Vishnu can alleviate. Vishnu has not yet manifested himself, but his presence pervades his heavenly resting place, the Ocean of Milk.

This remarkable painting stands at the beginning of the magnificent Mita Ram-Nana manuscript and hence also at the beginning of a great era of Indian painting. The painting's composition is as strong as it is freely rendered. Every brushstroke is alive. Each figure, moreover, is an animated individual, believably physical. All four of Brahma's heads rest comfortably on his shoulders. It is also fascinating to see how the artist has triumphed over the two-dimensional constraints of his tradition to create a dynamic grouping by ingenious overlapping. Thus, the herder boy's upper body appears in front of Indra, his lower body behind Indra.

The Earth-Cows of this and the preceding painting are virtually a distillation of the history of three centuries of Indian painting, one Earth-Cow embodying the vivid boldness of the early sixteenth century, the other the assured, expressive naturalism of the late eighteenth.

3. Narada, His *Vina* Resting on His Shoulder, is Received with Honor

Nurpur, c.1690 A.D. *The Brooklyn Museum (On loan from the Arthur W. Sackler Collections). 133 x 190 mm. Nurpur attribution made by Catherine Glynn.*

The subject of this painting is not indicated on the painting itself, but there are good reasons for supposing it to be a portrayal of Narada's meeting with Kamsa. Narada is traditionally credited with having invented the *vina* and is almost invariably shown holding one. He has been greeted by his august host with exceptional honor, just as described in the *Harivamsa's* account of this episode. The lotus that Narada offers Kamsa may suggest the heavenly secret he is about to divulge in gratitude for the courtesies shown him. Narada's beard is elegantly curled and trimmed, betraying the streak of vanity that Kamsa is successfully exploiting. Kamsa has not yet heard what the gods have in store for him, but a certain restlessness lurks beneath his apparent calm.

This handsome painting exemplifies the delightful blend of sophistication and sheer arbitrariness that characterizes many paintings from the Himalayan hills, particularly those dating from the second half of the seventeenth century. A flat background highlights the two boldly expressive trees draped with graceful vines, and the weird geometry of the two platforms provides a splendid foil for the delineation of these two grand but flawed personalities.

4. Devaki and Vasudeva Worship the Newborn Krishna Represented as Vishnu

North India, c.1570 A.D. From the Isarda manuscript. See also figures 25, 26 and 31. Edwin Binney, 3rd, Collection. 200 x 270 mm. Reproduced in Walter Spink, Krishnamandala, Ann Arbor, 1971, figure 11.

To the left, Vasudeva and Devaki are standing in adoration of their just-born son, who displays his eternal form as Vishnu and holds in his four hands Vishnu's emblems: lotus, discus, mace, and conch shell. The fact that Vasudeva and Devaki are Kamsa's captives is symbolized by coffered doors hung with chains. But Krishna's impending escape is foreshadowed in the fact that the guards and their dogs are asleep.

The *Harivamsa* provides no details of how Krishna was miraculously carried out of Kamsa's guarded palace and delivered into Nanda and Yasoda's care. The logistical ambiguities of this episode are explored and resolved only in later accounts. The *Bhagavata Purana* thus relates that, just as shown here, shortly after his birth Krishna manifests himself to his earthly parents as Vishnu. Vishnu then explains to Vasudeva that a mode of escape for Krishna has been arranged by the gods: the prison doors will swing open and the guards will be found sleeping. Because Vishnu instructs Vasudeva to take Krishna to Nanda and Yasoda, Vasudeva is, moreover, relieved of any moral responsibility in the subsequent slaying of Nanda and Yasoda's infant daughter. In the *Harivamsa*, in contrast, Krishna's ultimate identity remains concealed, and

the emotions Vasudeva feels as he strives to save his son from certain death are simply those of an understandably distraught human parent. On these very grounds, Andhaka seeks subsequently to excuse Vasudeva's actions (see page 78).

Whether or not he is believed to have been perceived by his parents as Vishnu, Krishna at birth is awe-inspiring. His body glows with dark brilliance, and the world is wondrously enhanced by his presence. The Isarda artist has captured the spirit of this transcendent moment in a movingly restrained manner. Vishnu's majesty is suggested principally by the huge lotus on which he sits, and by the graceful symmetry of his posture and taut scarves. Totally lacking in ostentation, the painting is a masterpiece of lyrical intensity. Delicate and symbolic, subtle and bold, it evokes a mood of awed exaltation.

5. Leaving Krishna with Yasoda, Vasudeva Returns to the Palace Carrying Nidra

Mankot, c.1730 A.D. Edwin Binney, 3rd, Collection. 286 x 210 mm. Reproduced in W. G. Archer and Edwin Binney, 3rd, Rajput Miniatures from the Collection of Edwin Binney, 3rd, Portland: Portland Art Museum, 1968, figure 54a.

Having placed Krishna beside Yasoda, Vasudeva sets out into the rainy night to bring Nidra to Devaki. The transfer occurs while Yasoda is sleeping after the exertions of birth, but the artist has chosen to show instead Yasoda's reaction upon awakening. Joyously she gives her breast to the child she believes she has just borne. A second woman presents Yasoda with auspicious tufts of grass, which will be placed beside two other such tufts on Yasoda's bed. Above Yasoda's head, an oil lamp glows in the darkness.

By juxtaposing these two contrasting moments, the artist has given the painting a muted, pensive quality. The viewer's inclination to respond to Yasoda's sense of fulfillment is arrested by an awareness that her daughter is being carried to her death. Ultimately, elation and sadness are both overwhelmed by an awed sense of the inexorable unfolding of a preordained drama.

116

6. Herder Women Admire the Baby Krishna

North India, c.1540 A.D. From the same manuscript as figures 2, 12, 14, 15, 18 and 27. Mr. and Mrs. Gordon Douglas, 3rd, Collection. 175 x 230 mm.

Krishna was reared in an extended family. Yasoda and Rohini lived together in the same compound, jointly raising their sons Krishna and Balarama. In a larger sense, all the herder band were Krishna's kin and all the other herder women shared Yasoda's maternal role. The *Harivamsa* gives considerable attention to these other women of the herder encampment. Their fascination with Krishna and their conflicted feelings of admiration and envy for Yasoda are characterized with great realism.

In this painting, Krishna's many mothers seem wondrously vivified simply by being in the presence of the mysterious dark child. The painting illustrates well the venturesome yet disciplined sense of composition of the painters of the Mita Ram-Nana manuscript. Within the constraints of a relatively flat, two-dimensional style, a tremendous sense of organized movement has been conveyed by the use of dramatic asymmetry. The women are individuals and wear garments with varied patterns, but their rhythmically coordinated movement cascades steadily forward toward the small focus of their love. Energy is everywhere apparent, in the rendition of the clouds, the trees, the tasseled awnings, and the river below. The mythical beast's head, which forms an ornamental bracket, holds a banner streaming straight out.

7. Putana is Drained of Life

Kangra, c.1790 A.D. Private Collection. 175 x 117 mm. Reproduced in Masterpieces of Asian Art II, *New York: Asia Society, 1970, figure 19.*

Two separate moments in the story are shown. First, as Krishna sucks insatiably at her breast, Putana begins to writhe with fear. Some time later, after Putana is dead, Krishna's cries awaken the herders and they crowd around to see. The demon wet nurse is unmistakably an inhuman monster, but at the same time her

death agony is touchingly believable. Putana's obvious helplessness to resist Krishna's untiring energy makes her almost pitiable. Yasoda is unhurried as she tenderly withdraws Krishna from Putana's breast. The other herders, too, seem awestruck but not frightened. One woman carries a cup of glowing coals to light her way, a reminder that the events depicted in this brightly lit painting take place at night.

The white-bearded man is presumably Nanda, who is frequently represented as an elderly person in contrast to Vasudeva, shown ordinarily, as in figure 5, in middle age. This is somewhat puzzling, since the *Harivamsa* makes no reference to Nanda's age, whereas Vasudeva is explicitly described at the time of Kamsa's death as an old man. Conceivably, Nanda and Yasoda came to be thought of as virtual grandparents as well as foster parents of Krishna, in order to mute the sense of loss they will feel when Krishna is restored to his original parents. Both Yasoda and Devaki are, of course, always young and beautiful, whatever their husbands' ages may be.

The fair-skinned, reddish-haired boy is probably not Balarama. The artist may have borrowed him from Europe, but not necessarily, because in the northwestern hill regions of India where Kangra is located, one occasionally encounters light-colored hair as well as light complexions.

Forms in this painting are subtly modeled, soft colors are employed, and the whole composition is suffused with elegance. Nonetheless, the painting crackles with tension. Thorn-sharp branches are visible among the old tree's new-green leaves, and while Putana wears the same colors as do the beautiful herder women, her clothes are large, frenzied splashes in a blank, geometrically defined space. With its dreamlike juxtaposition of ugliness and beauty, violence and meditative calm, this painting evokes superbly the mood of the *Harivamsa*'s story of Krishna's earthly career.

8. Yasoda Ponders a Strange Occurrence

Mankot, c.1700 A.D. From the same manuscript as figure 23. Chandigarh Museum (Mankot Raj Collection). 205 x 310 mm. Reproduced in W. G.

Archer, Indian Paintings from the Punjab Hills, *London: Sotheby, 1973, as Mankot 25(i).*

For Yasoda the excitement of the moment has passed. While her companion, her finger to her lips, is still merely amazed, Yasoda strives to find the deeper meaning of Krishna's miraculous escape from injury when the two ancient trees fell. In her mind's eye she can still see her son unharmed amidst the broken boughs, tied just as she had left him to a heavy wooden hourglass-shaped mortar in whose hollowed-out end grain was pounded. How did Krishna get out of their courtyard? Why did the trees fall? Why was Krishna not hurt? What can account for her son's mysterious difference?

In focusing on Yasoda's reaction, the artist has reduced the event itself to an oddly schematized pattern. Relying on the viewer's familiarity with the story, the artist has created strong symbolic images. For example, Yasoda would scarcely have used such a long rope to connect Krishna to the mortar. The massive tangle of rope at Krishna's feet nonetheless is a whimsical reminder of the mess of things that children can make. Also, instead of being shown broken and scattered, the two trees, slender as rods, cross dramatically behind's Krishna's head. Krishna's delightfully mischievous expression could easily deflate even the firmest maternal resolve to scold.

The two small figures set against the hot yellow background presumably are the two youths said in later versions of the story to have been cursed to confinement in the two trees until their release by Krishna.

9. The Herders Move to Vrindavana

Kangra, c.1780 A.D. From the same manuscript as figures 11 and 24. National Museum, New Delhi. 225 x 305 mm. Reproduced in W. G. Archer, Indian Paintings from the Punjab Hills, *London: Sotheby, 1973, as Kangra 36(ii).*

As the villagers approach Vrindavana, they discover that it abounds in good grass, shade trees, flowers, and birds, just as Krishna had said. Nanda directs the procession from his central canopied cart. In the second cart, Balarama and Krishna are seated with their foster mothers

Rohini and Yasoda. The children's outstretched arms remind us of their ultimate responsibility for the move underway.

A comparison of this painting with figure 10, which is closely related to it in theme, reveals the subtle transformation achieved by Hindu artists as they assimilated the naturalism introduced by Akbar. Like figure 10, this painting is an accurate record of landscape, implements, clothing, hair styles, and physiognomies. Telling details are numerous, and we are left with a sense of the artist's perfect understanding of the herders as distinct individuals. But the realist's commitment to individuation is balanced by the Hindu artist's fondness for dreamlike repetition, seen here, for example, in the two carts with their similar canopies and perfectly matched, but not identical, pairs of oxen. The result is a painting capable of leading the viewer steadily onward from a fascination with particular details toward a mood of reverie.

10. The Herders Set up Camp in Vrindavana

Mughal, c.1590 A.D. From Akbar's Harivamsa *manuscript. See also figures 13 and 28. Virginia Museum, Richmond. 298 x 187 mm.*

The herders have set to work, and in short order the new encampment is functioning smoothly. The amenities of settled life have already been restored, and as he returns to camp with Krishna and Balarama, Nanda is greeted by Yasoda with a tray of refreshments. Bulls and cows are happily exploring their new homeland, with their calves secured from predators behind a thorn hedge. Two women are returning from the riverbank with earthen pots on their heads. Two other women are busy churning and cooking. A propped-up cart is laden with tree branches brought from the forest. A framework of stout branches covered with woven mats provides shelter; since they were obliged periodically to move on when grass and firewood were exhausted, the herders preferred to use such simple constructions. Confining themselves to rough terrain unfit for tilling, the nomadic herders were free to make their camp where they wished. Such regions were inhabited otherwise only by wild beasts of the sort depicted in figure 15.

Although the conditions in which the herders live are what worldly persons might consider poor, when Krishna is with them the herders feel as fortunate as the immortals in Indra's paradise. Precisely this spirit has been captured by Akbar's imperial court artist. Far from appearing forbidding, the rugged landscape seems agreeably varied and colorful. The herders and their cattle are quite at home as they move sure-footedly about among the rocks and ridges.

11. The Herder Boys Enjoy the Rainy Season

Kangra, c.1780 A.D. From the same manuscript as figures 9 and 24. Bharat Kala Bhavan, Varanasi. 214 x 202 mm. Reproduced in Leigh Ashton, ed., The Art of India and Pakistan, *London, 1950, figure 565.*

Rains have brought renewed life to Vrindavana. Wildflowers spring up by the Yamuna's shore, vines are laden with blossoms. Cranes soar, a monkey perches in a tree. The tree on the right, draped with vines and with birds nesting in its branches, is probably the Bhandira fig tree, which is described in just these terms in the *Harivamsa.* Like this tree, the Bhandira fig tree is undoubtedly a "banyan," a tree celebrated for its broad crown and for the roots that grow downward from its branches. As Krishna plays his flute, the other herder boys race about marveling at the glories of the season. Their calves stroll or rest in the soft grass. Two herder boys and two peahens admiringly watch a peacock spread his wings and rear high his gleaming tail, which thrusts upward like a golden flame.

This painting is wonderfully detailed and colorful, but it is perhaps most remarkable in its evocation of sounds, scents, and motion. We can hear Krishna's lyric flute and the songs of excited birds. Above all, we sense the wind as it swirls moist and fragrant through the woods.

The painting's fragmentary character and the consequent impossibility of determining its original dimensions make its relationship to figures 9 and 24 uncertain. But an unskillful drawing, apparently a copy of this painting while it was still intact (reproduced as figure 5 in M. S. Randhawa, *Kangra Paintings of the*

Bhagavata Purana, New Delhi: National Museum, 1960), suggests that about one-third of the painting is now missing on the left-hand side; in its undamaged form, Krishna would have been near the center. If this clue can be trusted, the painting's original dimensions would have approximated those of figures 9 and 24. Archer does not list it along with figures 9 and 24 as being from the manuscript he calls "Kangra 36," but he does accept it as a painting done at Kangra (William G. Archer, *Indian Paintings from the Punjab Hills,* London: Sotheby, 1973, i, 269). At the very least, it is closely comparable to "Kangra 36" in style, date, and quality.

12. Krishna Subdues the Serpent King Kaliya

North India, c.1540 A.D. From the same manuscript as figures 2, 6, 14, 15, 18 and 27. Mr. and Mrs. Gordon Douglas, 3rd, Collection. 175 x 230 mm.

This action-packed painting tells an elaborate story. In the painting's main area, three scenes are depicted. First, Krishna, his scarves flying, is shown leaping nimbly from a Kadamba tree, with its fringe of lamp-like orange blossoms. Then Kaliya traps Krishna in his coils while Kaliya's sons seethe about, breathing forth flames. Finally, Krishna dances in triumph on Kaliya's head, displaying Vishnu's own conch in his left hand. Heavenly maidens hail his triumph. Two of Kaliya's "mermaid" wives plead that his life may be spared, and geese and lotuses reappear in the purified pool.

Three other scenes are depicted to the left. Above, Yasoda is informed that Krishna has leapt into Kaliya's pool. In the center, the thunderstruck Nanda receives the same message from Balarama. Below, cows and herders are being given an eyewitness account of what is transpiring in the pool by a herder who has climbed up the Kadamba tree for a better view.

The painting explodes in all directions, but at the same time it has been knit together by the recessing of the panel where Yasoda faints, and even more impressively by the figure of the herder halfway up the tree. The tree itself starts at the bottom of the page as a formal space divider and is then bent and expanded into a glowing central halo for Krishna's decisive leap.

The painting captures well the spirit of this crucial event in Krishna's earthly career. Indeed, the power and control evident in this splendid painting make it one of the most fully realized of all artistic expressions of the Krishna story.

13. Balarama Destroys the Ass Demon Dhenuka

Mughal, c.1590 A.D. From Akbar's Harivamsa *manuscript. See also figures 10 and 28. Los Angeles County Museum of Art (Nasli and Alice Heeramaneck Collection). 330 x 176 mm. Reproduced in Pratapaditya Pal,* The Classical Tradition in Rajput Painting, *New York: The Pierpont Morgan Library, 1978, figure 11.*

As Krishna and the other herders cheer him on, Balarama is preparing to send Dhenuka flying up among the fronds of the palmyra trees, which gleam with the luscious dark fruit sought by the two brothers. In the lower right corner, a pleased-looking herd of cows stands ready to take advantage of the new grazing ground that Balarama is making secure for them.

This painting combines strength of conception with extraordinary delicacy and refinement of execution. Trees and animals are depicted with scientific accuracy. Modeling and perspective have been employed expertly, and the viewer has a clear sense of all spatial relationships. In addition, a fine sense for pattern and design is evident in the line of flying birds, the gracefully curving palm fronds, and the clustered bunches of nuts on the ground, in the trees, and falling through the air. The almost impressionistic freedom with which the artist has rendered other details, such as the new-green foliage and the blood coughed up by Dhenuka, strengthens the impression that this is the work of a master. Pratapaditya Pal has suggested that the painting may be by Basawan, possibly the greatest of all Akbar painters.

14. Pralamba Carries off Balarama

North India, c.1540 A.D. From the same manu-script as figures 2, 6, 12, 15, 18 and 27. Private Collection. 175 x 230 mm. Reproduced in Indian Painting, *London: P. & D. Colnaghi, 1978, figure 46.*

Their jumping game concluded, the losers good-naturedly hoist the winners onto their shoulders. The demon Pralamba then reveals his true form, although, incongruously, the burly giant still wears his herder loincloth, anklets, and bracelets. As Pralamba begins to run away with him, Balarama gestures frantically and looks about for aid. Krishna, meanwhile, calmly prepares to restore Balarama to self-awareness by reminding him that he already possesses the strength within himself to destroy the demon.

Krishna's majestic reply to Balarama's plea for help is in a sense the real subject of this painting, and it is fascinating to see how the artist has deftly summed up a complex situation in such a way as to direct the viewer's attention to this fact. Thus, instead of gawking at the demon, the two herders in the center turn hopefully toward Krishna. In a simple gesture of tribute, a third herder holds a flowering branch over Krishna's head. Pralamba glowers apprehensively at Krishna. And though Balarama has turned away, his flying scarf, continuing the line of his upraised arm, points directly to Krishna's lips.

15. Krishna Hunts Animals Suitable for Sacrifice

North India, c.1540 A.D. From the same manu-script as figures 2, 6, 12, 14, 18 and 27. Temple Art Collection, New York. 175 x 230 mm.

Krishna here pursues a diversity of wild animals for a sacrificial feast. In ancient India cows were much too valuable to slaughter for food, but the flesh of other animals was often prepared as a delicacy on ritual occasions, such as the celebration of the Govardhana Hill, which Krishna initiated. This particular depiction of a hunt is actually an illustration of a later incident in Krishna's life, when a feast similar to the celebration of Govardhana is in preparation at Indraprashtra, located on the Yamuna upstream from Vrindavana. Arjuna is the bowman in this painting, while Krishna serves as his charioteer, just as he would do in the *Bhagavad Gita*. The woman seated in meditation to the left is probably Kalindi, a personification of the Yamuna River whom Krishna meets and marries following the hunt. (See J. M. Sanyal, trans., *The Srimad-Bhagvatam of Krishna-Dwaipayana Vyasa*, Delhi, 1973, chapter 58, page 230. I am grateful to Daniel Ehnbom for this reference.)

The complex subject matter of this painting is handled in a bold yet subtle fashion. Blocks of black, red, green, and yellow form an abstract design, emphasizing the distinctness of hill, forest, and plain. Plants and animals spanning these areas form the connecting links. A rabbit is poised in mid-jump between red and green. The twisting extension of a snake's tail penetrates the lower border. Also noteworthy is the artist's use of color accents to achieve an effect comparable to naturalistic modeling. Red slashes define the boars' bulk. The deep seams of the rhinoceros's hide are suggested by broad blue shading.

This painting appears to be a progenitor of a major genre of later Indian painting, the secular hunting scene. It may well have directly influenced the seventeenth- and eighteenth-century portrayals of maharajas hunting painted at places such as Kota. This painting shares with the finest of Kota painting an inspired capacity to empathize with wild animals, whether predator or prey.

16. The Herders Reverence the Govardhana Hill

Basohli, c.1760 A.D. Private Collection. 225 x 327 mm.

Krishna sits atop the Govardhana Hill as the hill's personification, and to the left Krishna can again be seen standing beside Balarama, joining in the herders' tribute to the hill. The herders and their cows are enjoying the festivities, their spirits buoyed by the sounds of drums and trumpets. But the religious character of the observance is also well conveyed by the upturned gaze of the figures to the left, and by the meditative mood of the young woman (Yasoda?) whose head is bowed. The procession is considerably more demure than is indicated in the *Harivamsa*, but the painting captures perfectly

the spirit of a community participating collectively in a joyous ritual. In keeping with the festival's egalitarian spirit, the barechested priest and the white-bearded patriarch (Nanda?) are simply part of the crowd. The artist has also drawn sharp portraits of many other distinctive individuals and grouped them with a sensitive attention to personality. In the center, for example, a man carries a child tenderly in one arm, and a woman rests her hand lovingly on a young boy's head.

This painting is from what W. G. Archer has labeled the "fifth" *Bhagavata* series from Basohli. (See Archer's *Indian Paintings from the Punjab Hills,* London: Sotheby, 1973, i, 49ff.) This series, together with the related "sixth" Basohli *Bhagavata*, represented by figure 1, forms an important link between the earlier and later styles of the Himalayan foothills. (For the earlier style, see figures 3, 5, 8 and 23; for the later, see figures 7, 9, 11, 19 and 24). The elaborate naturalism of later hill painting makes a tentative appearance in such details as the use of "rearview" perspective to convey a sense of three-dimensional movement around the hill, and the dramatically accentuated eyes of earlier hill paintings have been modified, anticipating the new lyricism.

17. Krishna Lifts the Govardhana Hill

Bundi, c.1640 A.D. Victoria and Albert Museum, London. 340 x 216 mm.

In accord with later versions of the story, Krishna gently supports the Govardhana Hill on the tip of the little finger of his left hand, treating the hill, in the *Harivamsa*'s words, with the solicitude one might show a favorite guest. Overhead, Indra's elephant Airavata continues his rampage through the sky. Rain plummets down and trees are blown about. But below the hill, all is green and peaceful. Two groups of cows, calves, and herders, familiarly intermingled, enjoy the hill's protection, while two smaller groups arrive to join them. One latecomer holds an umbrella cleverly fashioned from leaves. In amazement, Balarama points a finger to his lips, as do several herder women. But most of the herders seem more grateful than amazed at Krishna's accomplishment.

In certain of its compositional characteristics, such as its vertical format and elaborate grouping of figures, this painting seems indebted to Mughal prototypes. It is possible that the artist may have seen one or more of the versions of this subject painted for Akbar. (See, for example, the one contained in the Jaipur *Razm-Nama*, reproduced in T. H. Hendley, *Memorials of the Jeypore Exhibition*, 1883, iv, or the painting from Akbar's *Harivamsa* in the Metropolitan Museum of Art, New York, reproduced in Stuart C. Welch, *Imperial Mughal Painting*, New York, 1978, plate 10.) But other features of this painting from the Hindu court of Bundi in Rajasthan affirm its ties to Hindu prototypes. The "bead curtain" representation of rain traces back to paintings such as figure 4, and the segmented division of the riverbank could be traced even further back, through palm leaf paintings to ancient sculptural prototypes. Beyond such details, the painting's mood of reverence marks it as a work done within the living Hindu tradition. The artist shows little interest in giving a physical sense of what Krishna did, and seems primarily motivated to indicate the satisfaction that comes from contemplating Krishna's deed.

larger than the once mighty Indra, and the once fearsome Airavata has become a most obliging elephant. As is typical of this manuscript, the edges of the painting are frayed and there has been considerable flaking of white paint. Compensating for this loss is the opportunity it affords to study the artist's underdrawing.

In addition to the title *Govinda*, which might be translated "Indra of Cows," Indra cagily accords Krishna the title *Upendra*, "Indra the Second" or "Second to Indra," and mentions that in a previous life he was Krishna's older brother, as Balarama is in this life. Balarama and Indra, in fact, have much in common. Both are moon-colored and both are subject to fits of drunkenness, which distinguishes them from their composed, dark-skinned younger brother. Krishna's status as the younger brother of both Indra and Balarama, moreover, is an echo of religious history. Devotion to Krishna seems to have grown steadily in the centuries just preceding the beginning of the Christian era, as Indra and Balarama receded into the background from earlier positions of ritual superiority.

18. Indra Pays Homage to Krishna

North India, c.1540 A.D. From the same manuscript as figures 2, 6, 12, 14, 15 and 27. Private Collection. 175 x 230 mm. Reproduced in Stuart C. Welch and Milo C. Beach, Gods, Thrones, and Peacocks, New York: Asia Society, 1965, figure 3b.

Indra's four-tusked white elephant Airavata celebrates Krishna's consecration as *Govinda*, "Lord of Cows," by pouring water over him from a golden pot. "Thousand-eyed" Indra, identifiable by his pale skin as well as by the eyes painted on various parts of his body, is shown twice: prostrate at Krishna's feet and then addressing him respectfully. Overhead, gods join in the celebration, and from the left herders approach with garlands. But it is the tiny cow with head uplifted in her lower left-hand box who subtly dominates the composition, just as she is symbolically responsible for the event underway. Her champion, Krishna, is shown much

19. Krishna Distracts a Herder Girl

Guler, c.1790 A.D. Edwin Binney, 3rd, Collection. 184 x 114 mm. Reproduced in W.G. Archer and Edwin Binney, 3rd, Rajput Miniatures from the Collection of Edwin Binney, 3rd, Portland: Portland Art Museum, 1968, figure 85a.

Krishna's dalliance with the herder girls of Vrindavana has long been a popular theme of Indian poetry and painting. A religious metaphor capable of stimulating reflections about the relationship of every human being to God, Krishna's love play can be simultaneously appreciated as a bucolic romance of awakening youth. Over the centuries, countless illustrations of Krishna's amorous adventures have been produced. Since many of these paintings were done for princes, they often reflect a sumptuous ambience quite remote from the humble realities of life in a cowherd camp. This painting, in contrast, is relatively faithful to the facts of herder life. Both Krishna and the girl with whom he sports are unpretentiously attired, and the girl carries on her head a plain woven basket filled with ordinary clay pots. Instead of a garden or marble pavilion, the setting is an open field by a stream.

The artist has used clear, sunny colors to emphasize the boldness of Krishna's daring daylight tryst, and a gentle sense of humor is evident in the artist's handling of the girl's dilemma. With a smile she struggles to keep her clay pots from falling and thereby leaves herself otherwise vulnerable. Even the wrinkled old tree looking on seems to be straining with new life simply because Krishna is near.

20. Krishna's Glowing Countenance Reigns over the Quiet Nighttime

Mewar, c.1610 A.D. From the same manuscript as figure 22. Private Collection. 90 x 140 mm.

Overhead the new moon beams down a subdued light. Myriads of bright stars and wisps of white cloud fill the sky with life and movement. Below, trees are bursting forth with flowers and new green growth. The night air is fragrant, moist, and cool. Inexorably, all are drawn toward Krishna as the embodiment, perhaps even mysteriously the cause, of all that is wonderful about this season following the monsoon rains. A peacock, peahen, a deer, a gazelle, a tiger, and a bear join the three herder girls in rapt fascination with Krishna.

While figure 19 exemplifies the overtly erotic aspect of Krishna's sport with the girls of Vrindavana, this painting seems to emphasize its mystical side. The painting's context is nonetheless also highly erotic. The manuscript passage that accompanies the painting states that the herder girls are offering Krishna their upper garments, "marked by the saffron from their breasts," as a cushion. The artist has chosen to show Krishna seated on a large boulder, which is not mentioned in the text but to which our attention is particularly called by the fact that the word *sila*, "rock," is written on the boulder's side—a detail charmingly in keeping with the naive intensity of this deeply felt painting.

Stylistically, this painting from a recently discovered manuscript seems related to the Chawand series, painted in the state of Mewar in Rajasthan and dated 1605 A.D. Modest traces of Mughal influence are evident in the squarishness of the women's heads and perhaps most markedly in the softly naturalistic shading with which the birds and animals are rendered. (For a pre-Akbar comparison, see figure 15.) However, the casual directness with which the painter has used a block of red to distinguish Krishna from the night's darkness stems from the earlier Hindu tradition.

21. Gods and Demons Churn the Ocean

Mandi, c.1790 A.D. The Metropolitan Museum of Art, New York (Gift of Mr. and Mrs. Alvin N. Haas, 1977). 174 x 195 mm.

This painting celebrates the story of one of Vishnu's most comprehensive triumphs. He suggests the churning to the other gods; he helps the gods as they and the demons spin the mountain about, using the serpent Vasuki as a churning rope; he stabilizes the mountain from above; and he becomes a tortoise to serve as a basis for the spinning mountain. The churning tosses up the sun, the moon, the seven-headed horse Uchchaisravas who draws the sun's chariot, the four-tusked elephant Airavata, the wish-fulfilling cow Sarabhai and the wish-fulfilling tree Parijata, the goddess of wine Varuni, Vishnu's own consort Lakshmi, and the vessels containing the dread poison that Shiva drinks and *amarta*, the drink that bestows immortality. When the *amarta* is suddenly seized by the demons, Vishnu pretends to be a maiden, beguiles the demons, and wins back the *amarta*.

Vishnu, in other words, dominates this narrative from first to last, just as he presides over this painting from his lotus seat atop the spinning mountain. To the left, Shiva, with a necklace of skulls and a snake wrapped around his shoulders, helps Vishnu pull the snake's tail. To the right "thousand-eyed" Indra helps out two fearsome but nonetheless appealing demons. Overhead the sun and moon look down with frankly puzzled glances.

The levels of meaning in this story are numerous, but centrally the story tells of a massive creative turmoil, a sort of cosmic sexual act in which the phallic mountain stirs the ocean to yield up her treasures. Subconsciously, at least, the artist has this sense of the story very much in mind. The painting is engagingly direct in other respects as well. Thus, while disregarding the "logic" of the mountain's placement on the tortoise's back, the artist has at the same time made us acutely aware of the tortoise's personality. The snake, too, has been imaginatively handled by an artist of genuine sensitivity. Though not highly polished in execution, the painting is imbued with tenderness and reverence.

22. Kamsa Instructs Akrura to Bring Krishna and Balarama to Mathura

Mewar, c.1610 A.D. *From the same manuscript as figure 20. Alvin O. Bellak Collection. 110 x 150 mm.*

Firmly grasping Akrura's wrist, Kamsa draws him close to reveal his sinister plot. The king's anxiety is apparent. The other nobles whom Kamsa has summoned are also apprehensive. But Akrura remains composed because he perceives that Kamsa's scheme will backfire.

Each person in this painting betrays his emotions in a different way. Kamsa crouches forward. The fly-whisk bearer holds his left arm defensively across his chest. The bearded man looks frankly alarmed, and scarcely comfortable since he is wrapped around a post! The man sporting a long sword wrings his hands, while his companion crosses his arms awkwardly at the wrists. Small in scale and seemingly casual in execution, this unpretentious painting is a masterly psychological study.

23. Krishna Battles the Horse Demon Keshin

Mankot, c.1700 A.D. *From the same manuscript as figure 8. Chandigarh Museum (Mankot Raj Collection). 205 x 310 mm. Reproduced in W.G. Archer,* Indian Paintings from the Punjab Hills, *London: Sotheby, 1973, as Mankot 25(iii).*

With a candy-striped herder's staff as his only weapon, Krishna calmly takes on the man-eating horse. Keshin has bitten into Krishna's arm, only to feel the amazing force of Krishna's fist. From the impact Keshin's body seems to explode, releasing blood, saliva, and excrement.

The artist has made Keshin a recognizable horse, even a somewhat small horse. But his neck, nostrils, belly, and thighs have been subtly exaggerated, and his knife-like ears, electrically bristling mane, and balled-up tail, tapering to a point, are highly disturbing. Moreover, by compressing both figures within the margins of a claustrophobic space which seems as hot as the sun, the artist reminds us that one of the two combatants will not emerge alive.

24. Akrura Sees Krishna and Balarama in the Yamuna River

Kangra, c.1780 A.D. *From the same manuscript as figures 9 and 11. Gopi Krishna Kanoria Collection, Patna. 225 x 305 mm. Reproduced in M. S. Randhawa,* Kangra Paintings of the Bhagavata Purana, *New Delhi: National Museum, 1960, page 77.*

To the right, Krishna and Balarama are seated in Akrura's canopied horse-drawn chariot. In the distance to the left, Nanda heads for Mathura in a simple ox cart, accompanied by a number of younger cowherds. In the center, other herders are resting in the shade by the river, having laid aside their staffs and earthen pots of milk, which are neatly covered with cloths to defend against insects. Birds nestling in the trees complete the image of quiet well-being. Yet, against this peaceful backdrop, a momentous drama is occurring. Ducking under the water, Akrura sees Vishnu seated on the serpent Ananta. Then he sees Krishna and Balarama. Rising up, he gazes over to discover that Krishna and Balarama are still visible in his chariot. The tranquil setting thus becomes a reminder that moments of blinding individual insight are often intensely private events.

The painting's bold phalanx of stalwart trees, the wavy, almost parallel lines edging river and forest, and the careful grouping of figures all attest to the artist's strong sense of design.

25. Krishna Kills the King's Dyer

North India, c.1570 A.D. From the Isarda manuscript. See also figures 4, 26 and 31. Anita Spertus and Robert J. Holmgren Collection. 190 x 255 mm.

The story of Krishna's encounter with Kamsa's dyer is well summarized in this painting, despite its seeming lack of narrative or spatial coherence. Why, for example, are Krishna and Balarama rushing forward when the dyer has already lost his head? And what holds up the dyer's clothesline? Such questions are irrelevant. The painting sets its own terms and in these terms works brilliantly. Forceful assurance characterizes the advance of Krishna and Balarama. And by showing the dyer's headless body still standing, the artist reminds us how abruptly the dyer's arrogance was dealt with. There is pathos, moreover, in the illogical attempt of the dyer's wife to flee *through* the Yamuna. The artist's portrayal of the Yamuna itself contributes to the mood of crisis. With currents swirling and lotuses bizarrely enlarged, the river explodes upward almost at right angles. In contrast, in several more serene paintings from the Isarda manuscript the Yamuna flows in a gently sloping diagonal. (See Stuart C. Welch, *A Flower from Every Meadow*, New York: Asia Society, 1973, figure 7.)

The Isarda painter's fondness for elegant design can be seen in the stylish array of scarves hung out to dry, as well as in the stylization of the headless dyer's collar of trickling blood.

26. Krishna Raises up the Hunchback Maiden

North India, c.1570 A.D. From the Isarda manuscript. See also figures 4, 25 and 31. Gopi Krishna Kanoria Collection, Patna. 200 x 270 mm.

On the eve of his public confrontation with the tyrant, Krishna's nighttime foray has struck Kamsa's capital like a sudden gale. In rapid succession Krishna encounters three residents of Mathura: a dyer, a garland merchant, and a hunchback masseuse. Responding differently, one with arrogance, one with fear, one with love, each feels Krishna's impact. Here, the climactic moment when Krishna transforms the hunchback into a woman of flawless beauty is portrayed with grace and dignity. In one hand, the woman holds a pot of ointment. Her other hand rests at her side in trusting submission. To the left, Balarama calls the other herders' attention to what is occurring. The herders looking on are subdued, their stances balanced. Seemingly they have quickly comprehended the calm magnificence of Krishna's deed.

The artist has made an abstract pattern of the line of cloud and the starry sky. Then, a tasseled canopy abruptly separates sky from earth. The painting's composition is simple, almost stark, though details such as the patterns of textiles are rendered with lavish care. The painting's rigid compartmentalization and its use of alternating background colors are archaic touches, as is the way the canopy's tassel ends reverse colors as the background color is reversed. This formality of setting paradoxically succeeds in giving liveliness to the figures in the foreground, who move freely across the painting's flat surface.

27. Krishna Eludes the Elephant Demon Kuvalayapida

North India, c.1540 A.D. From the same manuscript as figures 2, 6, 12, 14, 15 and 18. R. K. Tandan Collection, Secunderabad. 175 x 230 mm.

Outside the entrance to Kamsa's grand arena, Krishna and Balarama encounter the foul-tempered Kuvalayapida. The elephant is quick and wily but he has never before dealt with such an antagonist as Krishna. Kuvalayapida's drivers gaze about in bewilderment, and Kamsa's guards watch with consternation as Krishna toys with the murderous beast. To the right, Balarama admires Krishna's agility. Below, teeming with ducks, geese, and lotuses, the Yamuna River flows past.

The artist who created this masterly black, pink-eared Kuvalayapida and probably also the splendid white, pink-eared Airavata of figure 18 knew from firsthand observation how wondrously agile and animated elephants can be. The artist understood not simply what elephants look like but what they are like, in all their diverse moods. The befuddled elephant's impotent rage is captured perfectly. Kuvalaya-pida's close-set eyes and pink trunk, his black scraggly hairs, clublike tail, and bulbous temples are all exaggerated but at the same time powerfully expressive. Bedecked with tassels, banners, and bells and sporting a colorful howdah, the stymied Kuvalayapida is a superb symbol of his royal master, whose own downfall is near.

28. Krishna Drags King Kamsa from His Throne

Mughal, c. 1590 A.D. From Akbar's Harivamsa *manuscript. See also figures 10 and 13. Victoria and Albert Museum, London (Lady Macnaghten Bequest). 323 x 204 mm. Reproduced in Robert Skelton, "Mughal Paintings from Harivamsa Manuscript," Victoria and Albert Museum Yearbook II, London, 1970, figure 2.*

As he mounts the steps of the royal platform, Krishna has seized Kamsa by the hair. Kamsa's crown can be seen flying toward the ground, near where Kamsa's brother lies, already slain by Balarama. Below, outside the gate, are sprawled the demon elephant and the two wrestlers Chanura and Mustika. On every side, spectators react to Kamsa's downfall with widely differing emotions. The women gesturing frantically in the special pavilion are no doubt courtesans. The more modest woman brushing away an anxious tear as she watches from the tower may perhaps be Krishna's mother, Devaki.

Akbar's artist has armed Balarama with a plow because later in his career Balarama sometimes used a plow as a weapon and therefore was called the "Plow-wielder." (Balarama seems to have been originally worshiped as an agricultural deity, before he became associated in popular thinking with the nomadic herders' hero, Krishna.) In other respects as well, the artist shows less interest in making his painting correspond to the narrative than in building a composition that works aesthetically. The wrestlers are thus placed outside the arena, and what would have been a vast amphitheatre is collapsed into a tight space framed by dramatic angles. As a result the painting's rich complexity is sharply disciplined to focus primary attention on Krishna's triumphant ascent.

29. Krishna's Heroic Deeds in the City of Mathura

Nathdwara, c. 1800 A.D. Doris Wiener Gallery, New York. Detail of painting on cloth. Size of entire painting: 2743 x 2591 mm. Entire painting reproduced in Walter M. Spink, Krishnamandala, *Ann Arbor, 1971, figure 17.*

Women are filling their water jugs from the Yamuna. A washerman is at work. Pleasure boats ply up and down. Fish leap and lotuses rise up from the silvery waters. Priests in a temple compound near the river present offerings to a Shiva *lingam*. The crescent-moon-shaped city, a bright jewel set amidst green fields, is obviously a prosperous and busy place. All seems serene until one notices that Krishna's heroic deeds in Mathura are presented as a sequence occurring along the city's main street, from the gate at the lower left to the multistory tower at the upper right. Outside the gate, Krishna quarrels with the king's dyer and one of his wives. Farther along, Krishna accepts the hunchback maiden's oils and the flower merchant's garlands. Closer to the royal precincts, Krishna encounters the demon elephant, and then Krishna and Balarama together take on the two wrestlers. Finally, Krishna ascends a flight of steps to seize Kamsa by the hair.

The artist evidently intends the painting to be a representation of Mathura after Kamsa has been killed, and probably of the Mathura of the artist's own day, because an image of Krishna installed for worship can be seen at the top center. In fact, this large painting on cloth undoubtedly adorned such a temple, perhaps one in Mathura itself. The painting thus commemorates the fact that centuries after Krishna's brief sojourn in Mathura, the acts he performed as he strode through Mathura's streets remain vivid memories.

30. Kamsa's Household Mourns His Death

Kangra, c.1810 A.D. Private Collection. 330 x 440 mm.

Kamsa's regal apparel is ripped in many places and threads from his garments strew the ground.

Blood flows from his mouth and from wounds on his body. Holding her son's head in her lap, the gray-haired queen glances at her husband, Ugrasena, who sadly brushes away a tear with the end of his shawl. To the right Ugrasena can be seen again, departing as requested by the queen to seek Krishna's permission to perform Kamsa's funeral rites. Many of Kamsa's wives in testimony to their grief have cast jeweled ornaments to the ground beside his fallen crown. Outside the arena, half-hidden figures mourn.

Forgetful of his evil deeds, Kamsa's household is absorbed in its personal loss. In contrast to the sense of openness achieved by the "bird's-eye" perspective of figure 29, here a close-to-the-ground perspective makes the mourners seem confined. One can scarcely see over the palace walls and, overhead, rooftops have been lopped off. In the foreground ropes supporting a tent wall stretch disturbingly out of the picture. For the moment, despair reigns. As Ugrasena leaves, he appears weak and unsteady. But Krishna will soon restore his strength and his crown. Appropriately, in figure 31 he is shown in vigorous middle age, ready once again to rule.

31. Krishna Restores Ugrasena As King of Mathura

North India, c. 1570 A.D. *From the Isarda manu-* *script. See also figures 4, 25 and 26. J. P. Goenka Collection, Calcutta. 200 x 270 mm.*

As Ugrasena reverently honors him, Krishna daubs Ugrasena's brow with a mark of sacramental paste taken from the cup held by Balarama. A ceremonial parasol and a yak-tail flywhisk, both emblems of royalty, are held by two attendants. Three other attendants play various musical instruments.

Krishna and Balarama are still wearing their herder loincloths in testimony to their continuing preference for a rustic life. But Ugrasena's attendants are shown as well-dressed nobles of scarcely less stature than the king. The king, or *raja,* of Mathura was the principal figure of a ruling clan, the Yadavas. But the modest *raja* of Mathura was properly only first among equals and was chosen by consensus, not by a strict rule of primogeniture. Kamsa had usurped the title of *raja* by force and made himself a cruel and self-sufficient tyrant who scorned the Yadavas' traditionally consultative style of governance. With Kamsa gone, Krishna readily secures the approval of the clan's elders to the restoration of Ugrasena's benign leadership.

This painting is in a style slightly different from that of the other Isarda paintings reproduced here. Physiques are more rounded, stances less angular. The style is well suited to a subdued, quietly elated conclusion.

About the Translation

Every translator has a distinctive purpose; mine has been to make the original Krishna story available in English in the most direct and accessible manner possible. Each of the four great Sanskrit works that focus on Krishna is outstanding in its own way. The *Bhagavad Gita* is notable for ethical insight, the *Bhagavata Purana* for devotional intensity, the *Gita Govinda* for lyric ecstasy. The *Harivamsa*'s unique strength is, I believe, its narrative vigor. It is traditionally described as a "supplement" to the epic *Mahabharata*, and in both date and style the *Harivamsa* does seem closer to the epics than to the later collections of religious lore, the *puranas*. Evidence of the use of archaic methods of oral composition can be found in the *Harivamsa*, and its message is conveyed exclusively through a fast-paced adventure story. Although it was clearly not composed by one person or at one time, the *Harivamsa*'s central section, the story of Young Krishna, is a wonderfully sustained and coherent tale. The poem's first and last sections, which briefly describe Vishnu's other incarnations and give a sketchy outline of Krishna's later life and of the lives of some of his descendants, seem less inspired.

The entire *Harivamsa* was twice translated into Western languages in the nineteenth century (into French in 1834 by M. A. Langlois and into English in 1897 by M. N. Dutt), but it was not until 1969 that a dependable critical edition of the Sanskrit text, prepared by P. L. Vaidya, was published by the Bhandarkar Oriental Research Institute, Poona, India. It is this text on which the present translation is based. Of the 118 chapters (6073 lines) constituting Vaidya's complete text, the central portion which has been translated here is about one-fourth (1544 lines). Included are lines 54-73 from Chapter 44, containing the description of Mathura before Krishna's birth, and the *Harivamsa*'s centerpiece, Chapters 46-78, beginning with Narada's visit to Kamsa and narrating Krishna's life from his birth until his triumph over Kamsa. From these chapters, two short passages together totaling 49 lines (Chapter 62, lines 68-99 and Chapter 67, lines 52-68), in which Indra and then Narada foretell Krishna's later adventures, have been omitted.

Acknowledgments

I feel a special indebtedness to Daniel H. H. Ingalls for introducing me to the *Harivamsa*. Professor Ingalls's discussion of the *Harivamsa*'s place in Sanskrit literature, "The *Harivamsa* as a *Mahakavya*," in *Mélanges d'indianisme à la memoire de Louis Renou* (Paris, 1968), was the initial inspiration for this work.

I am greatly indebted as well to my first mentor in the field of Indian painting, Stuart Cary Welch, whose passion for quality has never flagged; and to the late William G. Archer, truly a pioneer, whose enthusiasm for Krishna led him to take an active interest in this project.

Numerous other individuals have kindly shared with me in what could only be a mutual endeavor. Among these I wish to thank particularly Anil Arora, Milo Beach, Edwin Binney, 3rd, Thomas Burke, Gordon Douglas, 3rd, Daniel Ehnbom, Carolyn Elliott, Wendy Findlay, Klaus Gemming, J. P. Goenka, Michael Goedhuis, Catherine Glynn, Warren Ilchman, James Ivory, G. K. Kanoria, Tom Kessinger, Steven Kossak, Anand Krishna, Martin Lerner, Amy Poster, M. S. Randhawa, Robert Skelton, Anita Spertus, R. K. Tandan and Doris Wiener. The cooperation of the museum officials and private collectors who have permitted publication of paintings in their keeping has been indispensable and, moreover, offered with generous good will.

The following individuals and institutions courteously provided photographs, many of which were made expressly for this book: Anil Arora (figures 8, 23), Brooklyn Museum (3), Colnaghi (14), Colortek (29), Daniel Ehnbom (26, 27), Fogg Art Museum (18), Catherine Glynn (24, 31), Lorenzo Photographic Arts (4, 19), Los Angeles County Museum of Art (13), Metropolitan Museum of Art (21), Alfred A. Monner (5), Museum of Fine Arts, Boston (1), National Museum, New Delhi (9), Otto E. Nelson (2, 7), Eric Pollitzer (12, 15, 20), Standard Photo Service (22), Victoria and Albert Museum (17, 28), Virginia Museum (10), Herbert Vose (16), Doris Wiener (30).

YOUNG KRISHNA

was designed by Klaus Gemming, New Haven, Connecticut.
It was set by Mackenzie-Harris Corp., San Francisco, California,
in various sizes of Monotype Centaur, a twentieth-century typeface
by the distinguished American printer and designer Bruce Rogers.
The book was printed in four color process by
Princeton Polychrome Press, Princeton, New Jersey,
on Mohawk Superfine Softwhite 80 lb. text paper
made by Mohawk Paper Mills, Cohoes, New York, and bound by
Robert A. Burlen & Son, Inc., Hingham, Massachusetts.

THE AMARTA PRESS